A Workplace Story of an INPowering Life

Marcus Winn finds

A New Way to LEAD

6 principles of INPowering leadership everyone can use

Garland C. McWatters

Published by INPowered to LEAD Inc., Lewisville, TX
contact: mwinnbook@inpoweredtolead.com
972/762-3955

ISBN-13:
ISBN-10:

Printed by CreateSpace, An Amazon.com Company
Available from Amazon.com and other retail outlets
Available on Kindle and other devices

Marcus Winn: A workplace story of an INPowering Life
The series (so far)

Marcus Winn's Moment of Truth
Marcus Winn's Quest for Clarity
Marcus Winn Finds A New Way to Lead

Contents

Preface

LEADERSHIP happens upon us in different ways. Some seek to be leaders. Some evolve naturally into leadership roles as they assume larger management responsibilities. Others are thrust, perhaps unwillingly, into leadership roles and must figure it out under duress.

I tend to be one who seeks it out. The leadership bug bit early. I was elected reporter of my student council in the 9th grade. I continued to be active in student government throughout high school and college. As a young adult I held leadership positions in civic and professional organizations. Later, I was my party's nominee for the U.S. House of Representative (2000) in Oklahoma. Along the way, I have been in management and leadership positions professionally.

Through it all, I learned that leadership is more of an art than a science. There is not a single right way to lead. Neither is there a single list of skills and traits that make a perfect leader.

There is no shortage of leadership literature. Everyone seems to have a spin on what leadership is and how to do it. And to just about every leadership book I've ever read, I can say, "Right on."

But there is one constant I have come to believe: leading requires a willingness to connect with people.

Leading is a relationship, and like many relationships, we have to apply ourselves to making them work.

In this episode of *Marcus Winn's workplace story of an INPowering life*, our fictional protagonist finds himself evolving into a more visible leadership role as a new manager. This experience begins to open him up to new possibilities in his professional development.

I invite you to decide which aforementioned category of leader best fits Marcus's situation. Along the way, ask yourself how Marcus's experience can help you grow in your leadership ability. This story is relevant to all levels and types of leadership, regardless of management level, type of organization, years of experience, formal role related leader, or informal influencer of others.

I also invite you to open up to the idea that the most successful leaders are continually looking for *a new way to lead*.

Garland McWatters

Marcus Winn finds

A New Way to LEAD

1. Fighting words

The Color Run is billed as the happiest 5K run on the planet–a celebration of health, happiness, and community spirit. Marcus could not imagine how, on this third Saturday in April, he could be any happier as he crossed the finish line at Tulsa's Riverside Park, covered head to toe in green, purple, gold, and pink powdered paint.

AnnaMarie Flores had come from Springfield to run on his team. In the six months they had been seeing each other, Marcus had never seen her this playful as she jogged, skipped, and danced through the course. She slowed at each of the four color stations spaced along the course and took her time, squealing in delight, as the volunteers covered her in the powdered shade of that station. If a prize had been given for the most paint coverage head to toe, Anna and Marcus would have easily won. Everyone wanted to take their picture.

Carl and Steve, the other two members of Marcus's running team, were equally doused in paint. When Marcus first heard about the Color Run, he zeroed in on the word, "run," thinking it was an actual race. So, when they realized the Color Run was more of a fun run and not a timed event, they decided they would, instead, win by being the most thoroughly painted team to cross the finish line. Never mind it wasn't an official category. As far as they could tell, they were victorious.

Carl and Steve worked in the field at the company's Burns Flat wind farm and had become good friends with Marcus and his Tulsa team since Marcus had assumed leadership of the project. They made the four-hour trip to work with the team for a couple of days in the lab and to take advantage of Keystone Lake near-by. Carl pulled his bass boat, and Marcus roped them into running with a promise of a back yard cookout.

"Marcus. Marcus. Yoooo-hooo, Marcus." A high-pitched woman's voice called out from behind them. Everyone turned in unison to see who it was.

"Marcus. I thought that was you. You remember me, right? Beverly. Beverly Trudeau, the corporate public relations director."

"Oh, yeah," Marcus half-lied since he had never officially met her. "I got an email from you Monday about taking some pictures today for the *Derrick*," he recovered. The *Derrick* was the corporate online newsletter.

"Right. Glad you remembered. Not everyone did. My assistant is still rounding them up. Nice to finally meet you in person. I've heard a lot about you recently," Beverly extended her hand, and Marcus accepted her handshake. "I'm sorry I had to miss Mr. Johnstone's visit to your lab last month when he announced the funding for the all wind projects. You really made the oil and gas side stand up and take notice."

"So I've been told," Marcus tried to downplay the compliment and redirected Beverly. "And this is Steve Risner and Carl Westwood. They are part of the field team at Burns Flat wind farm," Marcus introduced them first.

Then he turned to Anna, "And this is Anna Flores, my girlfriend from Springfield. Anna's been my inspiration to get back into running shape. And she's a cousin to Erin Morales, my supervisor."

"Did Erin come out?" Beverly asked.

"No, she had a bunch of errands to do," Marcus explained.

"Well, I've asked my assistant to gather everyone representing Johnstone at the finish line for a group picture. Will you all join me over there?" Beverly nodded toward the arch designating the finish line. "You, too, Anna," she added.

The Color Run celebration concert was gathering momentum at the pavilion. A local rock band amped up the volume. Beverly shouted directions as she approached a group milling near the finish line. Obviously these were the other Johnstone Energy Enterprise entries. His team was the sole entry from the Millennium Energy branch of the JEE family tree that included Johnstone Oil & Gas, America's second largest independent energy company. Marcus did not know any of the participants personally, but some looked familiar.

"Hey, Marcus, I didn't recognize you at first," Elliot Sloan surprised Marcus from his right flank as he came up from behind.

Elliot had become Marcus's trusted mentor. Elliot seemed like an unlikely match since he was VP of Production for Johnstone Oil and Gas, but Erin suggested him when Marcus asked her for a mentor back in October to help him improve his supervisory skills. Elliot seemed to come up with ideas out of the blue that helped Marcus see situations in a different light.

Elliot's mentoring had a different feel to it than the hundreds of father-son talks he had with his dad over the years. Marcus knew he could rely on Elliot to help him navigate Johnstone Energy; he trusted his dad to help him navigate life. Marcus was thankful for the help on both fronts.

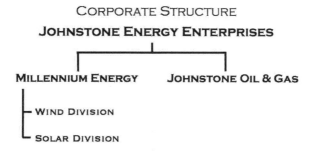

CORPORATE STRUCTURE
JOHNSTONE ENERGY ENTERPRISES

MILLENNIUM ENERGY   JOHNSTONE OIL & GAS

WIND DIVISION

SOLAR DIVISION

Marcus had missed the regular personal contact with his dad, whose engineering firm had sent him to a field office in Vermont several years ago. But now, his parents had returned to the company's headquarters in Joplin full time, and Marcus was looking forward to spending more time with them in the home where he had grown up.

In the spirit of the event, Elliot wore a Color Run shirt, but he did not have even a smidgen of paint on him.

"How'd you stay so clean?" Marcus greeted Elliot.

"Didn't run. Got better sense than that, but Jana and the girls did," Elliot nodded in their direction among the group under the finish arch. "Come on. I'll introduce you."

"Elliot, this is Anna Flores," Marcus half shouted over the music as he put his hand on Anna's back and positioned her face-to-face with Elliot.

"Marcus has told me so much about you," Elliot grinned. "It's nice to finally meet you. You look like you all really got into the spirit of the race."

"Marcus is a kid at heart," Anna beamed, putting her arm around Marcus.

"I think Beverly wants us to get this picture taken. I'll introduce you to my family when we're done," Elliot motioned to Beverly who was trying to get everyone arranged.

"Marcus, your team is obviously the most colorful. How about you four get in the middle, and we'll group the others around you," Beverly directed.

Beverly snapped several shots and announced she had what she wanted. The group quickly dispersed with most

heading toward the pavilion for the concert and the re-
freshment vendors—Carl and Steve among them.

Elliot brought his family to Marcus and Anna, "This
is my wife, Jana, and my step-daughters Nicole and
Hannah."

Jana stepped toward Marcus and gave him a one-
armed hug, "We were hoping to meet you, Marcus. Elliot
is very proud of what you've done as team supervisor.
Anna, it seems in the short time you've known Marcus
you've made quite an impression on him."

"He talks about Elliot a lot, too. I know he appreci-
ates the time and attention Elliot gives him," Anna returned the compliment.

"Listen, we've gotta run," Elliot interrupted. "The
girls need to clean up and get to a party later this evening."

"I hope it's as easy to clean this stuff off as the pro-
moters claim," Jana laughed and displayed her arms that
were nearly as caked with paint as were Anna's and Marcus's. "Nice meeting you both."

Marcus and Anna stood holding hands, facing the
pavilion, taking in the music and festivities. About that
time a burst of colors shot up from the crowd then settled
on everyone beneath. Marcus and Anna were just on the
fringe. A little more color would scarcely show up on their
caked skin and once white t-shirts.

"I didn't realize this would be so much fun," Marcus
looked down into Anna's almond eyes. "You are absolutely adorable in every conceivable way. On the list of
great days in my life, this ranks right up at the top.

Thanks for coming down. I know it wasn't easy to say, 'No,' to your new client this weekend, being a congressional candidate, and all."

"I had already made this commitment to you, Marcus. Besides, you're a higher priority than Eric Greer anyway," Anna turned and embraced Marcus with both arms.

A man's thin voice intruded into the moment.

"So, you're Marcus Winn." A lone man approached. He was one of the people Marcus recognized in the Johnstone group but didn't know a name.

Marcus and Anna released each other. Marcus turned to face the man who was now only a couple of paces from him. He also wore the event t-shirt, but looked like he had traveled the complete 5K circuit with minimal color damage.

"Yes. . . . Yes, I'm Marcus Winn." He wasn't sure to whom he spoke. "And you are?"

"Jim. Jim Bob Danner." He finished his name exactly as he stopped squarely about four feet in front of Marcus—no hand of friendship extended. "I prefer Jim Bob," he said placing both hands on his hips.

Marcus attempted cordiality, "So, you work at Johnstone, too?"

"Drilling."

"You look familiar." Marcus continued. "Maybe I've seen you in the cafeteria?"

Jim Bob appeared to be about Marcus's age—certainly not thirty yet. He was stocky, a couple of inches shorter than Marcus. Red hair covered thick forearms that be-

POWER: the ability to cause things to happen

SOURCES OF POWER

POSITION POWER: authority associated with one's title or position. Must be able to enforce demands.

REFERENT POWER: authority derived from affiliation with someone who has power. Might be delegated or usurped.

EXPERTISE POWER: authority one has because of skill or knowledge.

CELEBRITY POWER: authority one has because they are famous for any reason. Often asked to wield influence outside any personal expertise.

PERSONAL POWER: authority derived from one's strength of character.

came thick straight wrists on their way to massive hands and fingers tipped with well-chewed fingernails. It looked like his hair was growing back from an experiment with shaving his head. It was at the light fuzz stage so that as the sun backlit the top of his head, he looked slightly out of focus. His ears were thick and fleshy. His flat nose with wide nostrils sat atop thin lips, and his cleft chin anchored a round head. Jim Bob's eyes squinted when he talked, and opened when his mouth stopped moving.

"Maybe. I've noticed you sitting with that luscious blond several times," Jim Bob couldn't help adding as he glanced mischievously at Anna and eyed her quickly head to toe before looking back at Marcus.

"Yeah. That would be Teresa," Marcus offered.

"I know." Jim Bob cut in. "Everyone knows Teresa. A very friendly girl." Then glancing back at Anna, "If you know what I mean."

Marcus said nothing. He could see Anna glaring at Jim Bob.

"Just wanted to get a first hand look at a real life corporate celebrity. You cost me and my group a possible space expansion when you convinced Johnstone to save the wind projects. Everyone knows Johnstone's fascination with renewable energy is temporary. The real money is in oil and gas. Always has been, and will be for our lifetimes. No reason to throw good money after bad when we could make better use of it in drilling."

Marcus could feel the blood rushing to his head and Anna's grip tightening. His first urge was to lash out, and the muscles in his legs were tensing.

DON'T GET **Lured** INTO a Senseless ARGUMENT. **DEFLECT** PERSONAL BARBS. PUT UP YOUR EMOTIONAL SHIELD. **REDIRECT** INCOMING COMMENTS. **CLEARLY FOCUS** ON THE ISSUE BEING DISCUSSED.

Jim Bob kept it up, "Make all the fancy speeches you want. Oil and gas is the real winner here. Just sayin' it like it is."

Marcus could feel the hairs on the back of his neck bristle and his jaw tensing. All tells of his anger. Anna had never seen this side of him, the sudden rage, the urge to lash out. Marcus was sure the tips of his ears were flaming, because they felt hot from the inside out. The last thing he needed to do was make a scene. Marcus leaned forward toward Jim Bob to answer the challenge. Anna squeezed his hand tighter.

Marcus took the cue. He forced himself to glance over toward the side and release his confrontational stare. He tried to disguise how he was trying to quell the rising anger by taking a deep breath to relax the tension in his chest.

In his mind he could hear his supervisor, Erin, saying, *"Deflect and redirect. Deflect and redirect. Don't get suckered into an unwinnable argument. Deflect and redirect."* Marcus forced a half-smile as met Jim Bob's eyes, which had widened again since he stopped talking.

"Well, sounds like a challenge to me . . . Jimmy," Marcus spoke calmly. "I can hardly wait to see what happens next."

Jim Bob just smirked, "Humph. The only thing that counts is profits. And all I see is a pretty boy playing in the wind."

And with that volley, Jim Bob took a step back, looked Anna up and down again, turned, and swaggered into the crowd around the pavilion.

Marcus stood and glared stone-faced at Jim Bob's back. Anna stepped around in front of Marcus and took his other hand. "Come on. He's just an ignorant bully. I see guys like him all the time." Anna tugged down on Marcus's hands to make him look down at her. "Don't let him ruin this lovely day. I'm proud of you for keeping your cool. Now, let's go blow some of this dust off and head to Erin's. Carl and Steve know where to find us."

"Yeah, OK," Marcus smiled, looking into Anna's reassuring smile. "I'm sure you're right about him." But Marcus knew there were many other Jim Bob's rooting for Millennium Energy to fail.

Worse yet, Marcus had accepted an invitation to make a presentation at the corporate management retreat about his team's turn-around. The retreat was only a few weeks away, and he feared the audience would not be friendly, and he was lost for what to say.

2. Reality check

Marcus savored the freshly brewed chamomile tea, watching the Sunday April sky complete its nightly transition from a silver-blue to blue-gray and finally to lead-gray. With it, the temperature slipped into the low 60s—still comfortable for Marcus. He kept a slow, even rocking motion in the overstuffed patio swivel rocker. It had become such a natural motion over the years that he wasn't even aware of how precise its metronome-like rhythm had become—back and forth, back and forth, back and forth.

Marcus gazed over the inner courtyards from the second story balcony outside his bedroom that overlooked the quiet quadrille. The serenity of the place immediately captured Marcus the first time he walked into it almost two years earlier. It was similar to the peace he found on the expansive veranda at his sister, Lauren's home outside Springfield, where he went often for sanctuary and reflection. A garden club among the homeowners tended meticulously to the planning, planting, and care of the courtyard gardens. The labor of love was a win-win for everyone.

Anna had said her good-byes to Marcus and returned

to Springfield after lunch. Thoughts of his time with Anna flowed through his reverie.

Anna has captured me like no other woman I've ever known. She radiates confidence. She comes across as completely in charge of her life. The first time I watched her coach I was so taken by how grounded and balanced she seemed. Sure, no doubt she is exquisitely beautiful to me. It's impossible for me to keep my hands off her. But what captivates me is she just seems to know who she is.

I wish I could be with her every day. I hate being over two-and-a-half hours away. Maybe, if this relationship continues to deepen, she'll look for a law firm in Tulsa. I guess I can't expect that to happen right away. After all, she's getting more involved with the Greer congressional campaign, and that's going to take . . . Jeez, that's going to last another eighteen or nineteen months if he goes all the way to the general election. A month ago, when she first told me about it, the campaign seemed abstract; now it's getting more real.

I know we put off making any decisions about taking our relationship to the next level until June. I want to pour my heart out to her and tell her how deeply in love I'm falling. Then I catch myself, afraid I'll go and spoil it all by pushing too hard. What happens if June comes around and she's still not ready to move forward? Am I expecting too much from her too soon? It's just that I've become more clear in my own mind that I'm ready to think about settling down and building a life with someone. I want what Lauren and Jarod have in Springfield.

Now, things are happening at work. The team is coming together. My project is on solid footing with Mr. Johnstone's commitment to protect the funding. If I could just get a handle on this presentation I've got to make next month. I probably should not have agreed so quickly to do it. Should have thought it out. But when a vice president asks you to do something, it's hard to refuse.

Then you get a wise-ass like Jim Bob Danner in your face. Looking for a fight to show how tough he is. Who's he trying to impress? Does he think I'm intimidated? Insolent bastard! Wonder how many more like him there are that I'm going to have to deal with? Like Anna said, I should just shake it off. That makes this presentation all the more important.

Gerald Donovan, Millennium's R&D vice-president, put the wheels in motion for the presentation when he sat in on Marcus's interim performance review at the first of the year. Erin had shared Marcus's plan with Donovan about how he would improve his performance as a new supervisor. It looked impressive on paper, and when Marcus delivered on his plan and got his team on board, Donovan was eager to show off a Millennium success story to the entire Johnstone Enterprise management team.

Marcus's most recent triumph catapulted him into celebrity status around the corporate campus. His presentation to the corporate council that resulted in Nelson Johnstone committing the resources to continue all the Millennium projects, bordered on inspired, according to

Key points from Marcus's performance improvement suggestions to Erin Morales

Supervising is a lifestyle, not merely a job. Supervisors are entrusted with a leadership role. They must be:

- People oriented
- Clear minded
- Performance driven

Underlying principles

1. We live in a network of relationships. Each individually is personally responsible for the quality of those relationships.
2. Everything is personal, and everyone matters. Your work springs from the depths of your creative mind and spirit.
3. Everyone seeks personal meaning. We want to feel important and make a difference.
4. Everyone is personally accountable. We make choices and life and are responsible for their consequences.
5. Choose to be excellent to yourself and to others. Tell your truth kindly.
6. Change and diversity are life-giving processes. Embrace them.
7. Trust the force. These include motivation, love, and passion.

his fans. However, to some from the oil and gas side, it had been a sure bet the wind energy projects would be abandoned, since they had yet to generate profits. Nelson's announcement to the contrary stunned some of the senior managers who had never taken the alternative energy market seriously. No doubt, Marcus would be in the spotlight at the retreat.

I feel like I have a target pinned on my chest. Do I have what it takes to defend myself? After all, what does a twenty-eight-year-old wind engineer, novice supervisor have to say about leadership to managers who have been at this since before I was born? Why should they possibly take me seriously?

Self-reflection had become more a part of Marcus's temperament since discovering the new labyrinth in the park by the lake near Lauren's home last October. He had developed a habit of writing his thoughts on his tablet and reading back over them occasionally. But for now, he needed for the embedded image of Jim Bob's smirky insult to go away.

Marcus's phone chimed. It was a text from Jeannie Irwin, a teenage neighbor up the lake trail from Lauren, "Anna said u had a fun run. got caked n paint. what, no photos? u need a facebook page. seriously."

Anna, too, had befriended Jeannie, and was encouraging her to stay in Springfield after high school and go to community college, instead of leaving home just to get away from an unhappy relationship with her mom and step-dad, Kelly and Nick Tripp.

Lauren had taken an interest in Jeannie, which meant Jeannie had become a more natural guest in the Holman's home.

Each of these women, in her own way, had profoundly, yet unwittingly, contributed to his success during the past seven months. Lauren, the older sister, was the epitome of self-assurance, stability, focus, and calm. She had found a way to have a successful home-based business as a financial consultant to small businesses and be a stay-at-home mom. Anna, his love interest, who modeled successful coaching techniques with his nephew's soccer team, gave him insights into how he could better coach and direct his work team. Jeannie, a teenager in search of a life, had a way of holding Marcus accountable for his own success with her poignant insights about life.

OK, Marcus. Pull it together. I've got a team behind me. They'll help me get this presentation moving. Donovan wants to hear my ideas about leading and supervising. I guess I can start with what I promised Erin last October. Don't let a Neanderthal like Jim Bob Danner sucker me into useless egocentric arguments. Let Jim Bob's insult remind me that there are a lot of managers who need to hear about a better approach to leading. Now, if I can just find a way to explain it, and to understand it better myself.

* * *

Saturday's insult lingered. "A pretty boy playing in the wind," looped, with the image of Jim Bob's eyes squinting every time his lips moved, taking up the whole frame in in Marcus's mind. The churn in Marcus's gut translated into a sleepless night Sunday. He arrived by the 6:30 a.m. opening time Monday morning at the Black Gold Café on the main floor of Johnstone Enterprise's headquarters. Not even the cheery greeting from Mavis Harvey, the seventy-seven year old café manager, soothed the edginess.

Marcus caught his reflection in the floor-to-ceiling window as he took a table in the corner next to it, where he could be out of the traffic. The tops of the trees on the far side of the campus lake were just now catching the rising sun. He sat with his back to the café serving counter, powered up his tablet, and settled in.

"You cleaned up nice," Teresa Younger, who worked in the oil and gas land administration division stood next to Marcus's table, holding her tray of yogurt, a muffin, and a cup of coffee – her usual breakfast. "Do you always eat alone?"

Marcus, momentarily startled, looked up from his tablet. "Might seem that way, since you seem to always catch me like this."

"Mind if I join you?" Teresa slid the tray onto the table, assuming Marcus's permission, and sat. Teresa introduced herself into Marcus's life back in February. She had been straightforward about her attraction to him from the start. She lightened up when Marcus told her about Anna, but stayed in touch. "Were you looking at the group shot from the run? It's already posted on the *Der-*

rick. I wouldn't have recognized you except for the caption telling who was in the group."

"Do you know Jim Danner?" Marcus inquired.

"You mean Jim Bob? Yeah, I see him around. Why?"

"You might say he introduced himself at the run Saturday. Came up to me after the group photo op and insulted me in front of Anna."

"Insulted? How?" Teresa asked matter-of-factly as she pealed the top from her yogurt.

"Said I was a pretty boy just full of wind. That Millennium would surely fail and that what we do over there is meaningless. Then implied in front of Anna that I had something going with you. Stuff like that," Marcus explained.

"Yeah, that sounds like the Jim Bob I know," Teresa looked amused on the verge of laughing but held back.

Marcus noticed Teresa's amusement, "So you think that's funny?"

"No. Well, kind of, just a bit," then Teresa broke out in a grin and dropped her glance toward her tray.

"Well, I didn't like it at all. And if Anna hadn't been there to hold me back," Marcus paused. "If I hadn't of been able to restrain myself, there might have been a scene."

"You and Jim Bob in a scuffle!? Now, video of that would have gone viral," Teresa chuckled, unable to hold back her amusement, "And all colored up from the run. What a scene!"

"Well, he really pissed me off. What does he know?" Marcus was indignant.

"Listen, Marcus. Jim Bob is a lot of bluster. Now that you're more visible around here, and controversial, some people are going to take potshots. You've gotta develop a thicker skin and move on," Teresa advised.

"I'm only trying to do my job. I didn't ask for all this attention," Marcus protested.

"Goes with the territory." Teresa began peeling back the paper cup that held her muffin. "Back to my original question, do you always eat alone?" Teresa leaned back in her chair and waited.

"Most of the time, I guess," Marcus confessed.

"You've gotta get around more, Buzz," Teresa called Marcus by the nickname she gave him when word spread that he had impressed the corporate council with his presentation. "More people know your name since March, but not very many people know you. Heck, I wouldn't know you at all if I hadn't stepped up to introduce my-self."

"I get the point," Marcus tried to abort the topic.

"Relationships matter, Marcus, and it seems to me that yours are very limited. All I'm saying is let me intro-duce you to some of my friends. Maybe it's not as hostile on the oil and gas side as Jim Bob might lead you to be-lieve."

"I'll think about it. OK?" Marcus nodded.

"I usually eat lunch about 11:45. I'll be in the cafeteria with several of my friends. We're usually toward the far corner that looks out onto the patio," Teresa gathered herself preparing to leave.

The Burns Flat wind farm lab team

Team leader: Marcus Winn

Dan Packwood (senior engineer). 51. No ambition to be supervisor. Highly principled and quality conscious. Married, 4 kids ages 27-18. Masters Degree. Has been with Millennium Energy since it was formed in '04.

Sierra Trammel (engineer). 42. Widowed. 2 teenage children. Been with M.E. since '04. M.S. degree in environmental engineering.

Brad Skiver (engineer). 31. Single. BS degree. Started June '07 at M.E.

Carlos Alvarez (technician). 22. Single. Originally from San Antonio. Graduate of tech college wind energy technician program. Been with M.E. 21 months.

Miranda Evans (technician). 26. Lives with fiancé. Three years of college in electrical engineering. Dropped out to take care of aging parents. Been with M.E. 3 years.

Chris Daniels (technician). 36. Divorced. Single dad with two young children. Two years college and taking night classes at local university. Tulsa native.

Lori Ellis (technician). 33. Married with two sons. Learned welding and auto mechanics from dad and brothers in their auto repair business.

Sue Ann Lee (technician). 31. Married with five year old son. Expecting second child. Graduated in civil engineering from U California, Berkley. Moved to Tulsa with husband. Been at M.E. 3 ½ years.

Sanjar Banai (technician). 25. Single. Native of New York. B.S. Electrical Engineering. Graduated in three years. Been at M.E. July '09.

"Thanks for asking. Let's see how the morning goes. No promises today," Marcus admitted.

"Well, I'm easy to find, Buzz," Teresa stood and picked up her tray.

"I'll get that," Marcus grasped the corner of the tray and sat it back on the table. "Thanks for the advice."

"No charge." Teresa turned and made her way through the tables toward the cafe exit. Marcus watched her until she turned the corner toward the elevators, and returned his attention to his tablet.

* * *

The familiar aroma of the coffee waffling from the break area met Marcus when he opened the door to his project lab at 7:50 a.m. The banter of the team members discussing the weekend's activities caused Marcus to pause for a moment. He could pick out the voices just like he could pick out the voices of his family around the breakfast table.

The door opened behind Marcus. Brad, one of the team's three engineers, entered.

"Good morning, Brad," Marcus offered an upbeat greeting.

"Hey." Brad said flatly, limiting eye contact to a glance, and went directly to his office and flipped on the lights.

I wonder if I'll ever break through to Brad? Marcus thought, reflecting on the hit-and-miss contact he'd had with the junior engineer on his team since becoming team leader. Although Brad never voiced any specific resentment toward Marcus, common knowledge was that Brad expected to be promoted to supervisor, but Marcus was brought in instead. *There just always seems to be something in the tone of his voice, his aloof manner, and that vacant look in his eyes that keeps me from wanting to trust him.*

Marcus walked back to the break area, as he did most mornings, to brew a cup of herbal tea. The team members were still high from saving their Burns Flat wind farm project six weeks ago. The team had elevated its performance since learning the keys to being more clear about project expectations. The connections they had developed with other corporate departments during their quest for clarity were paying off with more effective and efficient work procedures and business processes. They had discovered some bottlenecks that they fixed with the involvement of vendors, as well as with internal partners.

Miranda Evans, a technician, was the first to see Marcus coming, "Morning, boss," she said straightening up. Everyone hushed and turned to look at Marcus. No one spoke. They were grinning and exchanging glances at each other like they had a secret.

"What?" Marcus picked up on the suspicious body language. He panned the group. Miranda, to the left, then techs Sanjar Banai, Sue Ann Lee, and Chris Daniels. Sierra Trammel, another engineer, stood beside Carlos Alvarez, the youngest tech on the team.

"What?" Marcus repeated.

Carlos nodded toward the cabinets behind Marcus.

Marcus turned to look, and the group erupted in laughter. The Color Run group photo had been copied and enlarged into a poster the width of the cabinet door. The added caption over the photo–reflecting the team's editorial comment–read, "Colorful leader of wind team puts Millennium Energy on corporate map."

Marcus turned back to the group, "OK, everyone. You give me way too much credit," Marcus couldn't help breaking into a wide smile. "You all did the work, and we are enjoying the rewards of that success."

"Yes, this is true, Marcus, and we know that," Sanjar interjected. "And even though we get our share of individual compliments, you are the team leader, and therefore, the one everyone recognizes. We are OK with that."

"I appreciate your confidence, and I'm trying to take all this in myself," Marcus answered, "but I don't fully understand everything that's happened, and I have been asked to talk about it at the company's leadership retreat next month. So, I need your help to get ready for the speech."

"Sure, Marcus, just tell us how we can help," Sue Ann offered.

"Yeah, whatever you need," Miranda joined.

"Have you asked Marcy Capshaw to help? I bet she would. She seemed really glad to help with our presentation to the corporate council," Sierra added.

"Possibly, Sierra. I hadn't thought about that," Marcus replied. "In the meantime, I will be asking all of you for some ideas soon."

A LEADER iS SUCCESSful ONLY IF the TEAM iS SUCCESSFUL !

"By the way, Marcus," Sanjar inquired, "we all know you've been seeing this lawyer from Springfield, Anna. But this picture is the best look we've had of her, and she's covered head to toe in paint. When are we going to meet her in person?"

A chorus of, "Yeah, when?" erupted from the group.

"I'm sure that day will come when it's time. Right now we're still getting to know each other better," Marcus assured. "Besides, you also know she's Erin's cousin, and I don't want to blow it with two women at the same time, especially when one of them is my boss."

Marcus turned to finish preparing his tea, and the others topped off their coffee before heading to their desks.

"I'll have more to say about my speech at the 8:30 huddle," Marcus let everyone leave the break area in front of him.

I hope I can keep this energy up for everyone. They deserve my best everyday, Marcus thought as he sipped his tea, glancing at the poster before turning toward his office.

* * *

Marcus arrived first for the huddle and took a seat at the far corner of the table in direct line of sight to the conference room door. He sat in different places around the table to avoid the notion that there was any single head seat reserved for the leader.

Marcus also was curious whether individual team members would sit next to the same people or mix it up.

So far, the only pattern he saw was for Brad and Carlos to sit together. Lori would either sit next to Brad or Carlos. Dan Packwood, the senior engineer, preferred the corner seat nearest the door. Everyone respected Dan's place.

The 8:30 a.m. huddle had become a team habit, almost a ritual, since the crisis in February around the funding presentation. Although Marcus had not set it as an official team meeting, the group had tacitly adopted it and just continued to show up for it every Monday morning. Sometimes it lasted only a few minutes, other times there was much to discuss. Marcus would at least summarize the team goals for the week and solicit topics. Today, Marcus wanted specific help.

"Good morning everyone. I hope you all had a relaxing weekend," Marcus began.

Miranda interjected, "Not as colorful as yours," she grinned and chuckled; others joined in.

Marcus continued, "We did have a blast at the Color Run. I didn't know it was possible to run and laugh so hard at the same time. And I think you all know that Risner and Westwood came up from Burns Flat to run with me–"

"And to fish Keystone," Sanjar jumped in, which brought outright laughter, because everyone knew Sanjar had been on the lake, twenty miles west of Tulsa, with them Sunday. He kept everyone informed of their catch on his Facebook page.

"And to fish Keystone," Marcus echoed through his own laughter.

Marcus continued, "Remember, Steve and Carl will be in this afternoon to brief us on their field work. They're prepared to stay over a couple of days if necessary. They both told me how impressed they are with this team. You make them, and everyone else at the wind farm, feel included in what goes on out of this lab."

Marcus paused. No one else spoke.

"Well, then, I have a special request," Marcus added. "I have been asked to speak to the management group at their leadership retreat next month. In light of our success, I want to get your ideas about what makes this group work well together. I want to give you some time to think about it, so in a couple of days I'm going to send you an email with several questions I'd like you to reply to. After that, I want to meet with each of you individually to get your critique of my performance as your team leader." Marcus paused and glanced around the table at the introspective expressions. "Is that OK with everyone?"

Most everyone nodded agreement. Brad looked down at his notebook and did not make eye contact with Marcus. Others exchanged glances along with their accepting nods.

Sue Ann spoke up, "Marcus, I have a suggestion." Marcus gave an approving glance for her to continue. "I think it would be helpful for us to have a formal staff debrief of the presentation project. It was an intense couple of weeks. I know we are proud of our accomplishment, but I wonder what we all learned from it as a group."

"Yeah, I think that would help me, since I'm the last one to come onto the team," Carlos jumped in.

Marcus took the cue, "So, what do the rest of you think about Sue Ann's suggestion?"

All enthusiastically supported the idea. Even Brad looked up and nodded his agreement. Dan Packwood, the senior engineer, gave Sue Ann a thumb's up gesture and a "that-a-girl" smile.

"Sounds like a 'Go,' then," Marcus concluded. "I think the sooner the better, so how about this Friday morning we convene at 10 o'clock in here. I'll have the café send up lunch. We'll work into the afternoon and call it quits for the week when we're done. Is everyone OK with that?"

Sue Ann beamed that her suggestion was so eagerly adopted.

"Anything else on that?" Marcus asked. No one spoke. "OK, then. Let's review our goals for the week before we break up."

*   *   *

The cafeteria was already filling at 11:50 a.m. as Marcus maneuvered his way toward the corner where Teresa said she would be. He felt like an intruder, the new kid at school being invited to the cool kids' table, unsure he would be welcomed. Teresa saw him coming and waved him over.

"Marcus, glad you could join us," Teresa's smile gave away her delighted surprise. She pointed to an available place at the round table. "Everyone, this is Marcus Winn, my friend from Millennium's wind division. You might have seen him in the group picture from the Color Run in today's Derrick. I invited him to join us whenever he could. I just didn't expect to see him so soon."

"Nice to see everyone," Marcus opened. "Thanks, Teresa, for inviting me."

The four others at the table introduced themselves in turn as Marcus took his place. Lily, who looked near retirement age, and also from land administration where Teresa worked; Chad, mid-thirties, a geologist; Sandy, probably late twenties, also a geologist; and Seth, who looked about the same age as Marcus, from marketing.

Seth and Sandy looked familiar, "I think I've met a couple of you before. Seth, Sandy, didn't I see you at Jazzy Jake's with Teresa back around the first of March?"

"Might have," Seth acknowledged, "I meet up there at least once a month with a group from work."

"Don't think we've met," Sandy looked like she was searching for a connection. "Think I would have remembered you."

"Marcus doesn't get out much," Teresa interrupted in a teasing tone, "It was all I could do to coax him into that one outing at Jake's."

"Well, I have been preoccupied with work," Marcus explained.

"It seems to be paying off. Your name has suddenly become well known around here," Lily said.

"The guy who single-handedly saved the wind energy division," Chad chimed in.

"You give me way too much credit," Marcus retreated, "Besides, I don't think Millennium was that close to extinction."

"To hear some tell it, your days were numbered until Nelson had a change of heart out of nowhere," Chad added.

"I think all we did was remind Mr. Johnstone why he got into the renewable energy business in the first place, and he decided not to give up on it yet," Marcus offered.

Sandy was curious, "And why did you choose wind energy, Marcus?"

"The Oklahoma City tornadoes in '99 fascinated me. When I saw on TV how powerful wind could be, I wondered if there was a way to harness all that power," Marcus explained. "Why did you all choose oil and gas?"

"Me?" Sandy answered, "I'm a rock hound, and geology and oil and gas are a good match."

"Then there's the money," Seth lightened up, "When times are good in oil and gas, the money is great, and right now things are really good."

Everyone laughed, and the conversation drifted into less serious topics. Soon, it was time to get back to work.

"Do you like to dance?" Sandy asked Marcus as they stood up to leave.

Teresa stepped in before Marcus could answer, "Down, girl. Marcus has a girlfriend in Springfield. I think he's off limits for now. " And she looked at Marcus, "Right?"

"Yeah. Right." Marcus smiled boyishly.

"Well, join us anytime," Chad offered. "We don't see much of the wind group, but we're really a friendly bunch, and we're easy to get to know."

"Sure. Will do. Thanks, and I'd like to show you all what we are doing sometime, Chad," Marcus said, "I think you would be impressed."

The group filed out toward the tray return. Teresa positioned herself in front of Marcus and slowed her pace. Then as the others had distanced themselves, she turned to face Marcus alone.

"That was a good first step, Marcus. I have a lot more friends I'd like you to meet," Teresa looked at Marcus expectantly. "Interested?" she asked.

"Yeah." Marcus hesitated then repeated, "Yeah. That felt good. I'm glad you prodded me."

"You'll be hearing from me soon, then," Teresa handed Marcus her tray. "Thanks for doing the dishes, again," and she turned toward the exit to catch her friends.

*   *   *

Marcus scanned the email one more time that he had drafted for his team over the last three days. With a click of the "send" button, he would make good on his promise from the Monday morning huddle to send out questions he wanted the individual team members to answer. Marcus thought through the rationale for his questions.

I want to know more about how they view themselves, not how they view me. I'll get that when I interview them individually. I don't want to ask them to put anything in writing that they might consider too sensitive. Plus, I want them to tell me something I might not otherwise know unless I asked. Since we are going to debrief the presentation project tomorrow, I'll have a chance to hear their thoughts on how we worked as a team. If anything comes out of that meeting that needs individual discussions, I can follow up later.

Marcus scanned the questions one more time.

- What are three things (factors) that motivate you to come to work everyday?
- What do you think is your single most outstanding strong point or talent? To what extent are you getting to use this talent in your work here?
- In what areas, professionally and/or personally, do you think you have grown in the past year?
- What are the three most important characteristics that you look for in a leader?
- In your own words, how would you state the mission of this project team? (Do not discuss this with other team members. I want to get an understanding of how unified we are in our perception. I will share the results with the entire team soon.)

Marcus added a deadline of Monday for their reply, and sent the email. His cell phone rang, and Anna's image popped onto the screen.

"Hello, Sweetheart," Marcus answered excitedly. "I didn't expect to hear from you in the middle of the day. What's up?"

"Well, I just found out that I've got to work this weekend, and I wanted to let you know so you could adjust your plans."

"Oh? OK. At least we can have dinner tomorrow night. I'm planning to get away from here a little early," Marcus replied.

"I'm sorry, Marcus, but that's not going to work out either. Greer's new campaign manager just called. They've scheduled a committee meeting for the weekend, and I have to leave with them tomorrow at noon. We won't be back until Sunday night."

"Be back? Where are you going?" Marcus rose from his chair and stood looking out the office window.

"Lake of the Ozarks. One of Eric's supporters has a lake home there and has offered to host the meeting," Anna explained.

"It seems kind of last minute." Marcus could not disguise his disappointment.

"I know. I was looking forward to seeing you this weekend, too. Things are starting to pick up with Eric's campaign, and there are some formalities we have to go over. You know, legal stuff," Anna explained apologetically.

"Yeah, sure. I understand."

"Are you still coming up to Lauren's?" Anna asked.

"Don't know now," Marcus hesitated. "Might just stay here and work on my presentation for the retreat."

"We can talk more tonight. I'll know more, and we can make some plans for the next weekend. OK?" Anna offered.

"OK. Usual time?"

"Yeah." Anna answered. "Right now, I've gotta go. I have a deposition in thirty-minutes, and I'm running a little late. Bye for now."

"OK, Sweetheart. Later." Marcus concluded.

Anna had already hung up.

Marcus stood gazing out the second-story window at the park across the boulevard. The redbuds, Oklahoma's state tree, signaled that spring was in full bloom. Marcus let his mind wander back to the Color Run five days earlier. Anna could make him feel light, alive, and carefree. That was the Anna he was falling in love with. But when she was focused on work, she could give him the impression that he was just a weekend distraction. Suddenly he had more free time than he had expected. He was in no hurry.

Hope this isn't a sign of things to come. Last minute trips and changes in plans. It's hard enough to have a distance relationship. Maybe after the campaign gets off the ground Anna won't have to be so directly involved. I so want Anna to be the one.

The desk phone warbled, jerking Marcus from his trance. He reached across the desk to grab up the handset before the call rolled to voice mail.

"Hello, this is Marcus."

"Marcus!" the voice was upbeat. Marcus recognized its gravel quality before it named itself. "This is Gerald Donovan."

"Hey, Mr. Donovan, what can I do for you?"

"Wanted to touch base about the retreat. I have an update."

"Sure. I was just thinking about my presentation."

"Good. Good. I know you'll be great. I've talked to our planning committee, and we have decided to move your presentation on Friday morning from the 9 o'clock slot to the 10:30 slot. That's one of the three prime time slots in the weekend. It sends a message about how important we think your topic is," Donovan explained.

"Will that change how long it's supposed to be?" Marcus asked.

"No, still thirty minutes for your comments, but it leaves more time for Q & A. We think there will be a lot of interest. At least, we're hoping there will be."

"Sounds like I'll be on the hot seat," Marcus quipped, trying not to expose just how anxious Donovan just made him feel.

"That's another thing I want to go over with you," Donovan continued. Marcus waited for him to explain. "We, the committee, would like to go over your key points with you ahead of time so we'll know how to support what you have to say. I think I know where you are coming from, but I'd like you to brief them on the key points you presented to Erin back in October. Would you be OK with that?"

"I suppose so," Marcus was apprehensive. "When would this meeting happen?"

"Middle of next week is what we're thinking. Could you be ready by then?" Donovan sounded like there was only one correct answer.

"I can work with that," Marcus agreed. *Like I have a choice.* "But I won't be finished. It'll be preliminary," Marcus hedged.

"That'll be OK. Coming from the Millennium side, I want this presentation to show the caliber of leadership we have coming up, Marcus. This is the first retreat where

Millennium has been anything but an afterthought," Donovan's excitement picked up.

"I'll give it my best, Mr. Donovan," was all Marcus could think to say.

"It's settled, then. I'll have Celeste contact you with the details. I'm thinking we'll meet Wednesday afternoon or Thursday," Donovan concluded.

"OK."

"And one thing more, Marcus. Cut this Mr. Donovan crap. I'm not your high school math teacher. Call me Gerald. OK?"

"OK."

Marcus heard a click, followed by the dial tone.

Great, Marcus. What kind of a mess have you gotten yourself into? All I want is to just do my job. Guess I know what I'll be doing this weekend after all.

3. Team debrief

S ue Ann beat Marcus to the conference room Friday morning. She had claimed the end chair with her back to the white board on the south wall.

"Good morning, Marcus," Sue Ann spoke first.

Marcus stopped without claiming a seat. "Good morning, Sue Ann. Looks like you got the jump on everyone."

"I've been looking forward to this meeting all week, and I have a request," Sue Ann said.

"OK."

"I haven't brought this up in our other conversations this week. I didn't know how direct to be with you, but I'd like to facilitate the meeting. At least the first part of it," Sue Ann looked up expectantly.

Marcus paused, thinking. *This is an interesting development. I've never seen Sue Ann so assertive. Does she think I'm not taking this debrief seriously? Let's go with it and see what she can do.*

"I think that's a great idea, Sue Ann," Marcus smiled, a bit surprised. "I'll just get things started and turn it over to you."

Sue Ann was always friendly and positive, but not particularly outgoing. Marcus was curious. "What prompted you to want to do this?"

"I'm a bit of an introvert, and I know if I'm going to advance in my career, I have to be able to present and command the attention of an audience. I decided it was time to try since this is a subject I feel strongly about and I know the project inside out," Sue Ann said.

"I'm impressed, and proud of you for taking the risk," Marcus added.

"This is as safe as it's ever going to be for me to try. The team is very supportive, and I know everyone will be for me," Sue Ann admitted.

"I'm certain of it, too," Marcus said. "I'll help any way I can. Otherwise, I'll just participate like everyone else."

I can only hope for a friendly crowd at the retreat. It took a lot of courage for Sue Ann to step out and ask. She's right. If not now, when? If not with this group, then which group? Maybe I'm creating my own fear factor with the retreat. I wonder if Elliot is available this weekend for a mentoring session?

With that, Sue Ann began to arrange the room. She set up flip charts and took out her notes. Obviously, she came prepared, intending to offer her ideas one way or another. Marcus walked next door to his office, tapping his phone's menus as he walked. He got Elliot's voice mail greeting, and waited his turn to speak.

"Elliot, this is Marcus. Can we meet at Hemingway's in the morning? I'm not going to Springfield after all. Let me know."

* * *

Lunch had come and gone from the Black Gold Café. The conference room walls were plastered with the team's notes from the presentation debriefing. Sue Ann had devised an approach that extracted even more information than Marcus had anticipated. Marcus made notes on both the lessons learned and on the techniques Sue Ann was using.

Surprisingly, Marcus found that allowing Sue Ann free reign as the discussion leader liberated him to engage differently. He was able to listen and observe in ways that leading the discussion himself would not have permitted.

I should invite others to lead team meetings. The group looks more relaxed, and they are talking more among themselves than when I ask them questions. I'd like to think I invite participation, but letting one of their teammates lead seems to make a difference in how openly they talk. Even when I ask tough questions it's less like I'm coming across argumentative and more like I'm sincerely exploring the issue. When I have my individual interviews with the group next week, I'm going to ask their impressions of this discussion, if they noticed the differences.

Sue Ann had organized the discussion into three major themes: (1) lessons learned about the Burns Flat project specifically, (2) lessons learned about working as a team, and (3) lessons learned about working within Johnstone Enterprises as an organization. She had further asked the team to discuss their experience of going from the surprise and angst over hearing their funding, and their jobs, might be in jeopardy, to focusing on solving the problem. She included a discussion about what they observed and learned by working closely together as a team under an urgent deadline in a crisis.

Marcus took specific note of three points the team members brought up.

1. They liked the open sharing of ideas and suggestions as they came up in their collaboration with each other;
2. They got to work on aspects of the presentation where they felt the most confident and able to contribute;
3. The serendipity they experienced as other topics and opportunities came up that had not been though of in their initial list of issues and challenges.

By 2:30 Sue Ann had summarized the results and gotten volunteers, Carlos and Chris–the youngest and the oldest techs on the team–to put their findings into a report everyone could access. Marcus was exuberant at the quality of the results, and the tone of the discussion.

"Before we dismiss, I want to congratulate all of you on a great discussion. I want to commend Sue Ann on a brilliant facilitation."

Then Marcus addressed her specifically as he stood at his place, "Sue Ann, you have impressed me beyond words today. I knew you were bright and creative, but I had no idea you could orchestrate such an involved discussion and command the room like you did today. Breaking the discussion into those three major themes kept us focused so we could get the most out of our time. You should have no reservations about your ability to facilitate any kind of session you put your mind to. You showed initiative and your willingness to take a risk: qualities we all can learn from. Thank you on behalf of all of us."Sanjar bolted up from his seat applauding. The rest of the team leapt to join the ovation. Marcus noticed Brad was the last to stand, and his applause was perfunctory. One-by-one each team member went up to congratulate Sue Ann. Except Brad, who gathered his notes and quietly left the room first.

"OK, everyone," Marcus talked above the hubbub, "That's a wrap on the week. If you want to leave early, you may. I look forward to your responses on Monday to the questions I sent out yesterday. I do want them in writing. Next week we'll schedule our private interviews. You did well today. Thank you."

Marcus went back to his office, trying to decide whether to leave or stay in the office until the end of the day. He had intended to head for Springfield as soon as he could get away, but those plans had changed with Anna's call. It dawned on Marcus that Anna was on her way at that very moment to her retreat at the Lake of the Ozarks with Eric Greer and his campaign team. This was the first time it had entered his mind since the debriefing had started that morning. Marcus didn't notice Dan Packwood, his senior engineer, standing in his doorway.

Dan cleared his throat to get Marcus's attention.

"Yeah, Dan. Sorry. Didn't notice you standing there. Come in."

Tips for giving positive feedback

Giving positive feedback acknowledges that one's actions have been noticed and appreciated for specific results. It affirms a desired behavior. The premise is that affirmation will encourage repeated good behavior.

The characteristics of a good feedback statement include:

- Comes from the feedback giver's point of view. The giver owns the observation.
- Describes the situation or action as a context for the feedback.
- Cites specific examples of the behavior.
- States the impact of the action.
- Links the behavior to a value or behavior that the feedback giver wants to recognize.

"You looked deep in thought."

"Momentarily on a mental trip, I guess. It happens sometimes." Marcus chuckled.

"I just wanted to stop in and tell you that you scored a lot of points with me today. Letting Sue Ann lead the meeting."

"Thanks, Dan. I appreciate that," Marcus noticed Dan was smiling, almost grinning.

"I think she has what it takes to be an engineer. I hope she gets the chance soon. This was a break through for her, and I appreciate you giving her a chance."

"She seemed determined to do it," Marcus added. "Did you, by any stretch of the imagination, have anything to do with making that happen?"

"A little, maybe," Dan grinned and looked down, then back into Marcus's eyes. "I see something special in her."

"You're a good man, Dan. I'm lucky to get to work with you. Thanks for your encouragement."

"My pleasure." Dan nodded once and disappeared from the doorway toward his office.

Marcus decided to stay in the office. He popped up his email. There were two new posts that caught his attention.

The first from Celeste. "Meeting next Thursday morning 9:30 a.m. with planning committee. Main executive conference room."

The second from Elliot, "Can meet in the morning early. 8? Too early for Hemingway's. How about the deli across the street from there? See you there unless I hear otherwise."

4. Crash course

The line inside the deli stretched half way to the front door through the crowed tables when Marcus entered. It was still a good five minutes before his meet up time with Elliot. *I didn't know so many people were up and around this early on Saturday.* Marcus panned the room for an available table. A hand waving from the back corner caught his attention.

Elliot was already there and sipping his coffee. Marcus waved back. Now that he was aware Elliot was waiting, Marcus was anxious for the line to move faster. *People stand in line for minutes, and when they get to the counter they haven't a clue what they want. What's with that?* Before he walked in, Marcus knew he would have a raisin bagel and a cup of lemon ginger tea. Five minutes later, Marcus took his order and dropped a dollar into the tip jar.

Elliot was leafing through the Tulsa World when Marcus finally reached the table. "Didn't know anyone still read the newspaper," Marcus said.

"Some habits are hard to break," Elliot started folding the paper up evenly as Marcus took his seat.

"Thanks for the impromptu session, Elliot."

"I thought you were going to Springfield this weekend. Your Anna is really charming. I can see why you are so smitten."

"She had to work through the weekend at the last minute. You know how lawyers are," Marcus did not care to go into the details. "As it turns out I need the time to work, too. Which is why I asked to meet you this morning. I could use a little reassurance."

"Tell me about it," Elliot invited Marcus to continue.

Marcus summarized his conversation with Gerald Donovan and Sue Ann's request to facilitate the debriefing. Elliot listened without interrupting.

"So, why do you think you need reassurance? Sounds to me like everything went pretty well," Elliot observed.

"Well, there's another situation that's been gnawing on me all week. I had a run in with a guy at the Color Run last week after you left. His name is Jim Danner, and he was quite a jerk to me in front of Anna," Marcus said.

"Yeah, I know who Jim Bob is. I'm not surprised," Elliot said.

"So, you know what I'm talking about then. He called me a pretty boy full of hot air, or something close to that. Everything in me wanted go jump him, but I kept telling myself, 'don't make a scene. It's not worth it.' And thank goodness Anna had a hold of me, too," both the pitch and volume of Marcus's voice rose as he told the story.

"I can tell he really pissed you off," Elliot looked amused.

"What's with it? You look just like another friend looked when I told them about Jim Bob. And they weren't surprised either. What's with that guy?"

"Jim Bob can be abrasive, but he's a hell of a driller. Just like his dad before him. Archie Danner is a legend among certain sectors of Johnstone. I knew Archie when I first came to Johnstone, and even had the pleasure of working with him. He taught me a lot about drilling, and I thought I pretty much knew it all," Elliot explained.

"So, that doesn't excuse him from being an asshole to me," Marcus stated indignantly.

"Did he say anything else?"

"Yeah, he said Millennium was a loser and that we were just wasting time and money."

"Do you believe that?"

"No. Hell, no. I really believe in what we're doing and that it will pay off for Johnstone," Marcus exclaimed.

"So, why the ire over what a driller says or thinks?" Elliot asked.

"It's just that I'm going into this presentation at the retreat, and Donovan said all eyes are on me to hold up Millennium's reputation. I wonder how many other Jim Bobs are going to be in the audience ready to jump me. And these guys are the leaders in the company!"

"Marcus, there will always be naysayers. No doubt, they can sound threatening. It's natural to get rattled when they start in on you. You have to learn to ignore the bluster and focus on your purpose. The worst thing that can happen to a leader is being ignored," Elliot said.

"Elliot, I didn't ask for this leadership role. I'm an engineer, and I just want to do my job."

"Here's a little reality check for you, Marcus. When you stepped into your position as a supervisor, your job fundamentally changed. You are more than an engineer now. You are a leader of engineers, and I think you have the ability to be a game changer for Millennium–like it or not. Erin, Gerald, me, and even Nelson Johnstone, we all see something special about you, and we want to be part of seeing what becomes of it. But, Marcus, you are the only one who can make it happen. The energy and power has to come from inside yourself. It's entirely your call." Elliot paused.

Marcus was staring into his cup as if the answers floated in there somewhere.

"Here's the question I'll put to you, Marcus," Elliot paused. Marcus looked into Elliot's eyes. "Who are you, Marcus, and how hot is the fire in your belly for what you do?"

Marcus wasn't quite sure what to make of the question. He sat quietly and glanced back into his cup.

Elliot continued. "Jim Bob Danner can come across as a jerk. He's pissed me off before, too. But the fire in his belly is drilling. His dad put it there, and everything that Archie was, Jim Bob will surpass. He's smart, tough, direct. He grew up in the roughneck culture, and that's what he will always be. But he is the kind of guy that, if he's your friend, he's loyal to a fault. You want people like that around you."

The **INPowered** take it upon themselves to **find ways to make things better** for themselves and others.

Garland C. McWatters

"Do you think he's right about Millennium? That it's a waste of time and money? That Nelson will give up on it?"

"Marcus, the only thing that matters is what you think and believe. Passion is infectious. Leaders lead. And the great ones develop new leaders to support their cause. If they don't, the cause dies with them. If you know who you are and where you are going, even those who disagree will respect you."

Marcus let Elliot's charge soak in for a moment. Elliot sat back and picked up his cup. It was empty.

"I'm going for a refill. Can I get you some more hot water?" Elliot offered.

"Yeah. Thanks. There's one more item on my list when you get back," Marcus said.

Marcus's phone buzzed. It was a text from Jeannie. "Lauren said u r not coming up. was hoping to c u. it's been 2 long since our last walk. next time?"

Marcus replied, "how about next weekend? I promise."

Then instantly, "ur on :)."

Elliot returned. "Now what's the other item on your agenda?"

"About this presentation. Do you think Marcy would help me prepare? Coach me?" Marcus asked.

"I would think so. I think you have her number. Ask?"

Marcus checked his contacts, "All I have is an email address."

"Start there, then. I know you impressed her, and she's worth whatever she charges," Elliot said.

"Thanks for the pep talk, Elliot. These conversations mean a lot to me."

"One more thing, Marcus. You won't be alone at the retreat. Erin will be there with all the execs from Millennium. I'll be there. Nelson is on your side. Sure, some of the guys are a bit cantankerous, but there are a lot of open minds. And, if I understand your topic, you are sharing your ideas about leadership, not the value of Millennium specifically. Right?"

"Right."

"That's a topic we all can learn from. You'll do fine." Elliot stood to leave."

* * *

Marcus laced his running shoes and selected one of the playlists of music he like to run to–about sixty minutes of high energy indie groups he collected from a variety of sources he could purchase online. He was stretching when his phone signaled an incoming email. *Marcy didn't waste any time getting back to me. Must not have much to do today.*

"Glad to help. Thought you had my number. Call asap at number below."

Marcus copied the number to Marcy's contact page and called it.

"Hello." Marcus recognized Marcy's voice.

"Marcy, this is Marcus. Thanks for replying so quickly," Marcus began.

"Sure thing. I'd be delighted to help you with your speech prep. Especially after the home run you hit with Nelson," Marcy said. "I think we should get started right away, if I got it right you've got about three weeks to get ready."

"Actually, I'm down to two weeks. I've got to be ready May the ninth. My slot is Friday morning."

"That's not even a full two weeks. Can you start this evening?" Marcy sounded urgent.

"I suppose. Whatever you say," Marcus was agreeable.

"Be at my place as early as you can. We don't have any time to spare. Bring everything you have prepared so far, notes, drafts, whatever, and we'll start getting the outline done. I'll text you my address. And clear your evening schedule until you leave for the retreat. OK?" Marcy ordered.

"OK. Will do. Is five o'clock soon enough?"

"I'll be waiting. And bring pizza. Supreme. Large. Thin crust."

"Done. See you at five sharp." Marcus hung up.

Marcus didn't have a thing on paper that he thought Marcy could use. No time for a full run right now. Better use my time to pull some ideas together this afternoon. Marcus checked the time. Not quite noon. I can still get in an up and back along the river. He set out on a thirty-minute run he calculated to end with a five-minute cool down walk back to his condo two blocks off Riverside Drive.

*   *   *

Marcus eased his 370Z through the winding, hilly streets of the upscale south Tulsa neighborhood of 4,000 square

"PASSION is infectious. Leaders lead. The GREAT ones develop new leaders to support their cause.

If you know WHO you are & WHERE you are going, even those who disagree will respect you."

Elliot Sloan

foot homes. He pulled into the drive for the address Marcy gave him. *Hope I got this right. GPS says this is the place.*

Marcus stepped onto the front porch. Before he rang the bell he could hear a husky bark announcing his arrival. The doorbell seemed redundant. Marcy answered quickly.

"Right on time. I like promptness," Marcy reached for the pizza box, "Come in, and don't mind Gus. It'll take him a few sniffs to get comfortable with you. He's the most lovable soul I've ever known."

Marcus dropped his hand so Gus, who looked like a mix between a bloodhound and lab, could sniff it. The lingering pizza smell required some extra sniffs. Once done, Gus panted a couple of times, and planted his haunches onto the tile floor, and raised his right paw to shake hands.

Marcus howled with delight as he knelt and took Gus's paw, "And hello to you, too, you handsome stud."

Marcy called from the kitchen, "Be careful what you say. Gus doesn't know he's been fixed."

"How did you teach him to do this?" Marcus's delightful surprise was obvious.

"Don't know how it happened. We taught him to shake, and somehow he thinks every time someone comes into the house, he's supposed to shake hands. Makes for a lousy watch dog," Marcy said walking back to the foyer.

"You have a lovely home."

"Thank you. But it gets lonely sometimes. All this room and no one to share it with," Marcy looked wistful for a split second. "But enough of that, you're here to work. Let's get down to it." She headed for the kitchen. "Thought we would work around the dining table instead of going back to the office."

Marcus followed. Gus trailed him. Marcy led them into a dining area that opened up into a larger den. The leather sofa and side chairs looked rich and inviting, but were not the oversized and stuffed style.

"So, I guess you have some ideas, Marcus? Show me what you've got." Marcy flipped open the pizza box and put slices on plates for her and Marcus, and opened the refrigerator door, "Beer?"

"Sure, why not?" Marcus agreed. He showed Marcy his notes about his principles of supervising that he originally gave Erin. He produced the notes he had made that afternoon—mostly ramblings about motivation, being clear about goals and results. He had even come up with an acrostic using the word, LEAD, to phrase some main points:

- Listen and learn
- Energize and engage
- Attend to the needs of others
- Determination and decisiveness

Marcy flipped through the notes. "OK, this shows you are thinking about the content, but it seems vague."

"I know. I'm getting some feedback from my team this week that I think will help me firm this up," Marcus explained.

"Good. We are going to need a central focus. Something your audience can remember. But these guys have heard a lot of leadership stuff. What's the one point that you want to make? If you only had time to make one point, what do you want them to walk out with?"

"I want them to respect Millennium, but I know that's not my topic."

"So, how else can they learn to respect Millennium?"

"I want them to accept us as a partner, and not an adversary. Not a stepchild," Marcus was firm.

"Good. We'll work that into the tone of the message, but it will be a subtext."

"Honestly, I'm feeling the pressure that if I don't do well, with all the hoopla I've received since the presentation to the corporate council, it will come back on Millennium. Donovan told me he wanted to showcase the quality of leadership coming up in Millennium. Frankly, I'm scared to death." Marcus confessed.

"You're right. That's a lot of pressure to carry," Marcy sympathized. "Marcus, I've worked with a lot of powerful CEO and political types, as well as many everyday people, and I've learned one thing that works across the board. This will work for you. I think it's the single most important piece of advice I can give. Ready?"

"Yeah. You've got my attention."

"It's not about you. It's about your story." Marcy paused to let her point sink in. "Lose yourself in your story, and you will forget what others are thinking about you personally."

"Hmmmm. I've never thought about that." The wheels were spinning in his mind.

"In the meantime, Marcus, while you are thinking about that, there are some technical things we can work on now."

"OK . . . coach. I'm in your hands."

"Stand for me." Marcy pointed to a spot a few steps into the den.

Marcus went to the spot and faced Marcy. "Like this?" He stood there with his arms hanging to his side. He felt conspicuous, and as Marcy eyed him up and down, Marcus began fidgeting with his hands, not sure what to do with them.

"We're going to work on posture and presence. I want you to command the space by the way you stand and move," Marcy explained. "People don't realize that most of the meaning they get from a presentation has nothing at all to do with the content of the message, but with the way it is presented. The way you look and sound, not specifically what you say."

"I never realized that," Marcus was curious.

"Don't get me wrong. Message counts, but the way you look and sound will make the difference on the impact of your presentation," Marcy elaborated, and stood to survey Marcus head to toe. "Good. You are athletic, trim, well proportioned. You're a nice height. About six, six-one?"

"Six foot even."

"We'll work on that slight slouch, then practice the way you move in the room and hold yourself," Marcy stood with her left arm crossed over her abdomen and tapping her dimpled chin with her right index finger.

For the next three hours Marcy put Marcus through a crash course of exercises to improve his posture, to help him project his voice, make eye contact with the audience, establish rapport, and gesture.

"I had no idea there was so much involved in making a speech," Marcus admitted when Marcy called an end to the evening.

"And we haven't even looked at the content yet," Marcy reminded.

"Is there anything I can be doing now to pull that together?" Marcus asked.

"Obviously you have a lot of ideas in the works. We need to shape them, like I said earlier. I have a speech format that I think might work for this one. Let me run back to my office and get it." Marcy headed down the hall leaving Marcus standing.

A framed photo caught Marcus's attention. An Oklahoma State college cheerleader sat on the knee of a uniformed Cowboys football player as he knelt on the turf. The scoreboard appeared above them showing the Cowboy's victory. The cheerleader looked like a younger Marcy. There were several other family pictures displayed around the den. Marcy with an older couple, likely her parents, Marcy with some children, several with Gus, and several couples photos of Marcy with the same man–her husband, Marcus supposed. Marcy returned to notice Marcus looking at the pictures.

"You were an OSU cheerleader?" Marcus asked when he noticed Marcy had returned.

"Go Pokes," Marcy affirmed.

"Me, too." Marcus said. "I mean, I'm a graduate, not a–" Marcy cut him off before he could finish explaining.

"I know. Class of '07. I've done some homework." Marcy picked up the photo and gazed at it, "The guy is Ted. We married the next year when we graduated. We both got PR and marketing degrees and moved to Tulsa. Ted went to work for the *World* in the sales department. Everyone loves a jock. I got a job with a small PR firm. Several years later we started our own PR firm. Had some early success. Got connected in Tulsa, and things grew from there. Before we knew it, we were in demand. My niche became image and speech coaching for executives and politicians." Marcy explained wistfully, without taking her eyes off the photo. Then paused and continued before Marcus could speak.

"Then Ted got sick. Five years ago. Without warning. Leukemia . . . AML, the worst kind. He didn't last a year." Marcy turned to Marcus. "After a couple of months of grieving, I decided I had a life to live, so I sucked it up and kept moving."

"I'm sorry for your loss."

"We never got around to starting a family. We liked being a power couple, and having children never became a priority. I have some wonderful nieces and nephews that I lavish my attention on. . . . And then, there's Gus."

"I can relate to the niece and nephew thing. My sister's kids."

"Anyway, Marcus, here's the outline." Marcy started toward the front door. "Look it over. I'll call you in the morning to set a time when we can continue this adventure."

"You can text."

"OK." Marcy opened the door.

"And good night to you, too, Gus." Marcus patted the ever-present companion on his head.

Marcy's speech coaching tips

1. The audience makes a judgement about you before you utter a word. First impressions of how you appear on stage create expectations. These non-verbals include:
   A. Posture: standing and walking
   B. Appropriate dress
   C. Poise
   D. Facial expression
   E. Establishing rapport and eye contact.

2. Lose yourself in your story (message),
   A. So you won't be preoccupied with yourself (the root cause of stage fright).
   B. This also will help you connect with your audience.
   C. Your presentation will be more natural and engaging, because you are having fun.

3. Write a solid presentation
   A. The main point of your speech or story.
   B. Three main points to support it.
   C. Give relevant, cogent facts to convince your audience.
   D. Include personal stories as appropriate to persuade your audience.
   E. Ask for action.

4. Practice
   A. Rehearse out loud to hear yourself say the words for emphasis and pacing.
   B. Be familiar enough with content that you don't need detailed notes. Don't read the speech.
   C. Know your content thoroughly, but don't memorize it word for word.

5. Straight talk

M arcus sifted through the emails returned by his team to the questions he had sent the previous Thursday. When Marcus got back from lunch he found an envelope on his desk containing Brad's response. As promised, Sue Ann, Carlos, and Chris had compiled the results of Friday's debriefing and sent everyone on the team a copy. Marcus was eager to read them and decided to stay late in the office for some quiet time before meeting Marcy for a work session over dinner. She had business near the JEE campus and thought that would be more convenient than having Marcus drive all the way to her place.

Marcus was eager to talk to Anna at their usual 9:30 p.m. phone rendezvous. They had not talked since the previous Thursday, but she had occasionally texted just to say she was too busy to talk during her trip. Anna texted him at 7:00 that morning to say she was already at her office and looked forward to their conversation later tonight.

I hope this isn't a sign of things to come. When we are so busy that we don't even have time to talk on the phone. I don't have good feelings about this. Anyway, I know Marcy will want to see what I've come up with for the speech. Sunday's session with her was interesting. I didn't expect her to quiz me about my wardrobe. Now she wants me to let a fashion consultant do a make over. Marcy is bringing someone named Reggie Thomas with her to dinner. This is starting to feel like one of those reality shows where strangers come in and rework your life. What have I gotten myself into? Oh, well. What can it hurt? Taking them over to my place after dinner.

Marcus skimmed the emails again and decided to create a matrix of the team's responses for quick reference.

OK. Let's begin sorting this out.

Several minutes later, Marcus stared at the matrix and the insights it revealed. *I hope everyone is being straight up with me on their responses. But I don't know why they wouldn't. This will give me a starting place for my individual conversations with them this week.*

An incoming message chimed in. Marcy. "still on for 6:30 at Persimmon Tree?"

Marcus checked the time. 5:50. He confirmed with Marcy and turned his attention back to the summary he was compiling. When it came to motivators, Marcus noticed a number of recurring themes expressed in slightly different words. He decided to group them accordingly. Sometimes two different themes were expressed in the same statement.

List of motivators, and the number of times mentioned:

1. Solving tricky or difficult problems (4)
2. Relating to getting to contribute, make a difference, use my talent (4)

3. Some form of working with talented people, being around smart people, teammates (4)
4. Learning and growing (4)
5. Doing a good job, best work, or right way (3)
6. Interesting work (3)
7. Paycheck (2)
8. Improving quality and doing things right (2)
9. Expressing myself, try my ideas (2)
10. Work on something important
11. Acknowledgement for my contributions
12. Fun

List of characteristics preferred in a leader. These were more straightforward. Marcus listed them verbatim.

1. Fair (4)
2. Decisive (3)
3. Integrity (2)
4. Visionary (2)
5. Has a plan, planner (2)
6. Encouraging, supportive (2)
7. Teacher
8. Protects the team
9. Problem solver
10. Committed to quality
11. Stands up for principles
12. Dedication
13. Good communicator
14. Clear
15. Open minded
16. Understanding
17. Trusting
18. Encourages innovation
19. Team builder

I guess, I see the team telling me that if I can be this kind of a leader for them and provide this kind of a motivating environment, we should have an effective team. This should interest Marcy.

Time to leave. Marcus gathered his papers and left for the Persimmon Tree.

* * *

Marcus closed the front door of his townhouse after saying good night to Marcy and Reggie. Marcus was astounded that there was so much research into how colors affected the way people reacted. Reggie was as well versed in that science as Marcus was in his understanding of generating electricity with wind power. Reggie's assessment concluded that Marcus's wardrobe could use a makeover. They would meet Thursday afternoon at four o'clock to shop.

Marcus brewed a cup of herbal tea—a blend of chamomile blossoms and peppermint—because of the late hour, and because he wanted to feel relaxed when he called Anna in a few minutes. He took his tea to the living room, kicked off his shoes, softened the lighting, and settled into his recliner. A sip of tea, a deep breath, and call.

Anna picked up on the first ring, "Hi, Marcus, I've been waiting for your call. I almost called you first. I've missed you."

"I've missed you, too, Sweetheart. It feels like an eternity since we talked last," Marcus said.

"I know. The last four days have been a blur. I haven't had a quiet moment. Politics is a lot more complicated than I ever imagined," Anna said.

"I was so disappointed when you had to waive off the weekend with me, but as it turned out, I needed the time down here to prepare for the management retreat."

"Are you about ready?" Anna asked.

"Not hardly. I didn't know there could be so much involved. I met with the PR consultant who helped my team prep in March. She put me through all kinds of exercise to help me have a more powerful presence in the room, as she called it. We're starting on the content tomorrow, and she hooked me up with a fashion consultant who just finished digging through my closet to evaluate my wardrobe."

"Now, I would have enjoyed watching you watch some strange lady going through your clothes telling you how you ought to dress," Anna giggled.

"Not a lady; a guy," Marcus corrected Anna. "Reggie. And he seems to know his stuff."

"Who's the PR consultant?"

"Marcy Capshaw. Elliot put us together."

"Marcy Capshaw? Her name came up this weekend in our meetings," Anna sounded surprised.

"How so?"

"As an image and speech consultant from this area who is good at working with politicians and business leaders. Zander, the campaign manager, mentioned her, then said he wanted Eric to use a consultant out of Atlanta who has worked with top Fortune 100 executives,

Team responses to Marcus's question:

"What do you think is your single most outstanding strong point or talent?"

Dan Packwood : Teaching others.

Sierra Trammel: Technical knowledge.

Brad Skiver: Precision and attention to detail.

Carlos Alvarez: Technical knowledge and a desire to do a good job.

Miranda Evans: Technical knowledge. Sociable.

Chris Daniels Seeing different ways to do things. Open to taking risks.

Lori Ellis Fast learner. Curious.

Sue Ann Lee Seeing alternative solutions to problems.

Sanjar Banai: Helping people find happiness. Giving encouragement.

and candidates for the U.S. Congress, the Senate, and governorships across the south."

"Well, I'm not running for an office. Just want to make a good speech at the company leadership retreat next week," Marcus downplayed it.

"All the same, it sounds like you're taking this seriously."

"I had an eye opening talk with Elliot Saturday morning. He told me I had stepped into a high visibility role in Johnstone, like it or not. Then Donovan told me my presentation would be in one of the showcase time slots. Marcy is helping, but I admit I'm on edge over this. I'm really looking forward to a little snuggle time with you this weekend to calm me," Marcus suddenly turned playful.

"About that," Anna's tone flattened. "I'll only have Friday night this weekend. I'm working Saturday with a big political law firm Zander is bringing in to be the lead. Our firm isn't big enough to handle all the details, but Eric insists that we be involved for local reasons, and that I be the point person here."

"I guess I'll take what I can get, but I was hoping for more," the disappointment seeped into Marcus's tone. "I'm coming up anyway because Jeannie texted me about walking the lake with her Saturday, and I said I would."

"I haven't had much contact with Jeannie lately," Anna confessed. "We keep missing each other. I hope I'm not letting her down. Besides, I think she's spending more time at your sister's."

"Really? Lauren hasn't said anything about that."

"I think she's stayed some with Andy and Susie while Lauren and Jarod get a little more couple's time," Anna added.

"How do you see this campaign affecting our time together?" Marcus hoped he didn't come across needy.

"I think I'll know more after this weekend. I'm hoping that I'll be able to do most of my work during the week. It depends on the rest of my load. You know how the partners expect associates to bill a ton of hours and bring in new business if they expect to make partner some day," Anna said.

"What's your take on Greer? Do you think he can win on his first try?" Marcus asked.

"No doubt he's got the fire in the belly, so to speak. He has a way about him that is almost hypnotic. When he's in the room, all eyes are on him. He seems to have some great ideas about this part of the state and what he can do in Congress to help. So I guess we'll see," Anna sounded mesmerized herself when she spoke of him.

"What do you think is so compelling about his story that people would want to vote for him?"

"He speaks clearly about three things he wants to accomplish: education, economic opportunity, and equality. He has a specific initiative to support each one, and he can explain them so that you can see yourself in his story. He's an amazing storyteller."

"Sounds like you're already a true believer," Marcus added.

"I hope you get a chance to meet him, Marcus. I think you would be impressed. He's only thirty-three. A successful entrepreneur, and he's been highly visible in the community for several years. I'm surprised at the reach of his network. He seems to know everyone."

"A family man?"

"A fiancé . . . Renee."

"I'm glad you have this opportunity, Sweetheart. I just don't want to lose any of the limited precious time I have with you. Especially with June the first around the corner." Marcus hoped Anna picked up on the meaning of the reference.

She did. "I haven't forgotten. You know, Marcus, June the first was an arbitrary date—not set in concrete. I just don't want us to rush into an intimate relationship that changes everything prematurely. We both have a lot going on."

"I get that. For me the more I'm with you, the deeper my affections run. I'm even nervous about using the 'L' word with you, although I think about you all the time, can't wait to hear your voice again, or to hold you when we're together, and for me, that's not often enough." Marcus caught himself pushing. "Damn, I'm sounding needy and possessive, and I promised myself I wouldn't go there." Marcus stopped."

"Marcus," Anna paused. "Marcus, listen to me. I'm not putting you off because I don't have similar feelings for you, because I do. I'm just saying, this kind of a commitment probably takes longer for me to make than it does for you. There are other things to consider beyond getting

Anna's three impressions of Eric Greer

1. *He has a* **PRESENCE**, *"When he's in the room, all eyes are on him."*

2. *He has* **PASSION** *for what he believes, "No doubt, he's got the fire in the belly."*

3. *His message is* **CLEAR**, *"He speaks clearly about three things he wants to accomplish. . . . He has a specific initiative to support each one, and he can explain them so you can see yourself in his story."*

involved sexually. How will this affect our careers, our families? What about the distance? And there are still issues we haven't addressed, namely my faith. I was raised a devout Catholic. I became disillusioned under the previous Pope, but Pope Francis has renewed my interest, and I want to get back to practicing my faith like I did as a teen. I mean, is that going to cause any problems?"

Marcus sighed deeply. Anna could hear it.

"Marcus, have faith that this will work out between us as it's supposed to. Let's not force it. Let's enjoy each other and see where this goes. I think there will come a day when we will both know when it's time. Don't you?"

"I respect where you're coming from, Anna. I don't want to seem like I'm pressuring you. I'm just hoping to move forward with my life before too many more years slip away. I don't want to wake up when I'm thirty-five or forty, and realize I just didn't get around to having a family."

"I understand," Anna reassured Marcus. "I'm sure that isn't going to happen to you." Anna paused. "In the meantime, we still have Friday night to look forward to. Will you be here by six?"

"I can make that happen."

"Good, I'll bring in dinner, and we'll have a quiet evening at my place. OK?"

"OK. Sweet dreams."

Marcus went to brew another cup of tea.

6. A dance lesson

T he countdown was on. Marcus looked forward to a
   couple of days in Springfield. He was eager to see
Anna tonight, and he promised Jeannie a walk around
the lake tomorrow. By this time next week, it would be all
over. In the meantime, the opening dinner of the annual
Johnstone Energy Enterprises management leadership
retreat would be served at 7:00 p.m. on the coming
Thursday. The company booked more than half of the
Phoenix Hotel resort at Grand Lake for the event. The
memo said more than 150 corporate executives, vice
presidents, their direct reports, plus spouses and plus-
ones would be there.

The daily retreat sessions would be held at the
Wilkes House, a stately mansion nestled on a heavily
wooded lake point. Once the secluded getaway for the
Oklahoma industrialist, Hubbard Wilkes, his family
foundation now operated the property as an exclusive
resort retreat. The mansion included ten sleeping rooms
with mingle and meeting space to accommodate day
groups of up to 100, ample for the JEE group.

The sleeping rooms at the Wilkes House would be
occupied by Nelson Johnstone; Nelson's daughter and
son-in-law, Lizzy and Travis Frisk; Wally Pierce, the

Chief Strategy Officer for JEE; Randall Allenbaugh, CFO; Cody Watkins, COO for NJ Oil & Gas; Tony Preston, President and COO for Millennium Energy; Tom Hayes, Sr. Legal Counsel; and three guests, usually featured presenters at the retreat. Marcus Winn learned Friday that he would be one of those.

Marcy and Reggie told Marcus during Thursday's shopping spree how much they were impressed with his progress. They would nail down the presentation content Monday night, rehearse on Tuesday, and have a dress rehearsal on Wednesday night. Marcy insisted it would help Marcus to speak one time before a live audience. She took it on herself to prepare a reception for a few close friends she wanted him to meet anyway. She promised they would be, "friendlies."

Reggie did his part to make sure Marcus had a wardrobe appropriate to his opportunity. Fabrics should be natural–polyester is taboo–and of the highest quality that Marcus could afford. Everything must be fitted to Marcus's athletic physique, moderately conservative, but fashionable for a twenty-eight year old professional from the heartland. Reggie was amused that Marcus would treat himself to a $2000 fashion wristwatch and wear it with $99 shoes. "Something's gotta be done about your footwear," Reggie gasped.

This is much more intense than I expected, Marcus thought, reflecting on what he had been put through in just one week, and Marcy wasn't through with him yet. *This is probably what my mother has been preaching for years when she talked about practice, preparation, and performance. All that work that must be done before the curtain goes up or the band takes the stage. I guess it's not too different from the hours of training I would put in before a cross-country race. I just never thought of applying that to making a speech. I always thought public speakers just had a natural knack for it. When I get back to Tulsa Sunday night I better have something solid ready to go for Marcy.*

Anna found Marcus's accounting of his week amusing, as they relaxed that evening in the comfort of her apartment. As promised, Anna was completely focused on Marcus and never brought up Eric Greer or anything about her work. However, Anna was very curious about what was happening with Marcus and his presentation.

"Sounds like Marcy has plans for you," Anna said.

"I think I'm more like a blank canvas to her, and she's getting to work from scratch," Marcus replied.

"From what I hear, she's one of the best, so do as she says," Anna encouraged.

Then Anna's tone softened, "You'll be wonderful," she whispered in his ear and shifter her weight, inviting Marcus to cuddle her on the sofa.

"This is what I've been needing," Marcus whispered.

"Me, too," Anna pulled Marcus's arms tightly around her.

Conversation stopped, and they just lay there cuddling. Marcus could feel Anna's body relax against him as she dozed off in his arms.

Marcus savored every moment. *This is as it should be,* he thought.

* * *

Marcus finally got to Lauren's lake home close to mid-
night. Everyone had gone to bed. He woke wide-eyed and
energized at 6:00 a.m. Not his usual Saturday morning
habit, as he often slept in until after 8:00 a.m. He made
his way through the quiet house to his favorite chair on
the expansive veranda looking out onto the community
lake, sipping tea, and thinking about what was in store
the coming week.

*Finding out I would be staying in the Wilkes House
blew my mind. I was content to show up, make my speech,
and listen in on what the management team talked about
at these kinds of event. Thank goodness I have Marcy's
help, I would be in so over my head. Probably still am. At
least I'm confident I have a chance to make a good impression. Still nervous about being in some hostile territory
thinking back on Jim Bob's attack. At least the people I've
met through Teresa at lunch seem friendly. She usually
has a couple of new faces at the table each time I've joined
her. Wonder if that's usual for her, or if she made that
happen for me? Probably usual for her.*

*The individual meetings with my team this week were
helpful and affirming. I expected them to be a little more
critical. I really do believe I'm making progress learning
how to lead them, and to understand that being in this
leadership role is way different than I imagined when I
took it. Talk about being thrown into the deep end and being forced to sink-or-swim. Thankfully, Erin got me on the
right track when she did.*

Sue Ann was a pleasant surprise. She told me what a boost letting her facilitate the debriefing was to her self-esteem and confidence.

Several of the techs said they would like more freedom to pursue solutions to technical issues without waiting for the engineers to give them permission. They thought there was some skill and talent in the group going to waste. Maybe I could loosen things up someway. I need to find out more about what they mean by this. I don't know why they think they have to hold back. Sounds like a topic for the huddle–suggestions for how to encourage and allow more autonomy.

Speaking of holding back, Brad always seems to be holding something in. He isn't overtly disruptive or insubordinate. I just sense he is harboring some deep resentment toward me. I'm eventually going to have to bring it up with him privately, but I'm not even confident he would level with me anyway. I don't want to make matters worse, but I know I'll have to deal with him, sooner or later. I think several of the team noticed he had nothing to say to Sue Ann after the debriefing. I certainly noticed it.

I still don't know how to bundle all this information to make a speech of it. What's that one thing I want the leadership of Johnstone to take with them? Glad I'm here for the weekend. There always seems to be some inspirational breakthrough when I'm here.

"Uncle Mark! You're here," Andy's greeting hit Marcus from behind as he bolted out the back door. Andy was hugging Marcus around the shoulders before he could stand up.

Marcus positioned Andy in front of his chair, "Here, stand up straight for me. Want to see what a just-turned-ten-year old looks like."

"Yep, the twenty-second," Andy said proudly.

"Sorry I didn't make it up last weekend. Work. Did you get the package I sent?" Marcus asked.

"Yes. The art pencils are great. I've never had a whole set like that," Andy beamed.

"Your mom told me you were wanting some."

"Jeannie's been showing me some things about shading and using color," Andy said.

"So, you've been spending more time with Jeannie?" Marcus inquired.

"Not a lot. She stays with us some when mom and dad go out. I really, really, like her," Andy admitted.

"More than Anna?" Marcus spoke before he thought.

Andy paused, puzzled by the question. "No. . . . Not more. . . . Different. Anna's my coach. Jeannie's my friend."

"She's my friend, too." Marcus hugged Andy, eager to change the subject.

"Morning, boys," Lauren stepped onto the veranda in her floor length robe and fur lined house slippers. "You're up early. Aren't you chilly out here?"

"Let's go in, and I'll fix pancakes for us," Marcus offered.

Before long, Jarod, Lauren's husband, and Susie, their soon-to-be-a-teenager daughter appeared in the kitchen. Marcus loved Saturday morning breakfast at Lauren's. The smells, the banter, the laughter, the love.

Marcus looked over the scene at the breakfast table. *Someday I'll enjoy this kind of a Saturday morning in my own home. Someday.*

"Lauren says you have a big presentation coming up this week at work," Jarod said.

"Yeah. Been working hard on it. Got some good help. Came up to get my thoughts together," Marcus answered.

"This place has a way of helping," Jarod said proudly.

"Right about that. . . .You know how I love this place," Marcus said emphatically.

"Now that your parents have moved back to Joplin permanently, I guess you'll be spending more time there, instead of coming here so often?"

"Some, I guess." Marcus admitted. "But coming here is like being on vacation for me. It has a unique energy I find . . . reviving. I don't think you are going to get rid of me that easily." Marcus laughed.

Marcus answered the usual questions about work and about him and Anna. In short order, the Saturday morning routine set in, and Marcus went back to his notes, and to getting ready for his promised walk around the lake with Jeannie.

A text from Jeannie, "meet u on the trail behind ur place at 10?"

"OK," Marcus replied.

* * *

Marcus sat on the bench next to the lake trail, waiting. Jeannie came briskly around the bend through the natural arbor of branches that spanned the trail shielding the view from where Marcus sat. He stood as soon as he saw her, and Jeannie jogged the last few steps and trapped Marcus's arms to his side in an embrace.

"I'm so glad you made time for me," Jeannie released Marcus and stepped back. "I don't get to see you enough."

"I'm happy to see you, too, Jeannie."

Her red hair was pulled back in a ponytail–usual for their walks. She wore grey compression capris, a long sleeve orange pullover with the OSU brand logo, and a white windbreaker.

"Did you wear that for me?" Marcus quipped.

"Glad you noticed," Jeannie grinned, spinning around once like a model. "How about we walk around the lake clockwise this time instead of the other way?"

"Now, that's breaking an old habit of mine, you know," Marcus said. "I can't remember the last time I went this way. I've always gone counter-clockwise so I could sprint across the dam at the end."

"Well, sometimes, change is good," Jeannie started walking. Marcus caught up.

"Catch me up." Marcus started. "What's been happening in Jeannie's world?"

"Jeannie's world has been . . . improving," Jeannie looked up and smiled.

"In what ways?"

"As you know, I graduate high school next month. You should get something in the mail about it soon."

"We'll be there. In force," Marcus promised.

"Starting the Tuesday after Memorial Day I go to work full time at Ms. Rippetoe's dance studio. I'm so excited. My first full time job," Jeannie clapped her open palms several times rapidly in excitement.

"Fist bump that," Marcus held out his left fist. Jeannie bumped it with her right one.

"The drama has settled down at home. Mom is still in her own world. Everything is about her, and I might as well be invisible. Nick (Jeannie's stepdad) still creeps me out the way he looks at me. Don't think that will ever change. Johnny's coming around, though. I changed my attitude and behavior toward him."

"How so?"

"Something I picked up from your family. I noticed how much attention your family members give each other and with how much love everyone treats everyone else. At first I was resentful toward my mom that we didn't have that. Then I decided if it's ever going to be different with my little brother, I had to do something different. I started being kinder to Johnny, starting conversations with him, paying attention to what's going on in his life, and now he's treating me totally different," Jeannie explained.

"Have you tried that on your mom?" Marcus asked.

"Not yet. I'm working up to it."

"Are you still planning to enroll in college?"

"I've applied for admission. Should hear any day. I have picked out my first classes that can transfer to a four-year college later. I'm good to go," Jeannie reported excitedly.

"Do you have many friends?" Marcus changed directions.

"Sure, silly. I'm not a wallflower," Jeannie seemed surprised Marcus would ask. "If you were on Facebook, you could keep up with me better." Jeannie gave Marcus a friendly bump with her left shoulder against his arm. "You'd be surprised how many people stay in touch that way, and how many new friends you end up having."

"Guess I've had my head in my work too much," Marcus begged off.

"Before we quit today, I'll help you get set up. You can do it on your phone then do all the extra profile stuff later."

"I don't know . . ." Marcus hedged.

"Oh, come on. It'll be fun. I just can't believe you aren't in on social media. Everyone does it."

"We'll see," Marcus still wasn't sure.

Jeannie took the conversational reigns. "And tell me about the latest in Marcus world."

"I've got a big speech to make this Friday at my company's leadership retreat. I've been concentrating on getting it ready."

"Wow, I'm impressed. Who'll be there?"

"All the company execs, V-Ps, and top managers from all divisions."

"What's the topic?"

"Leadership and my experience of learning to be a supervisor?"

"Leadership? What did you do to get that gig?" Jeannie exclaimed.

"My team made a presentation to our corporate council to save our project funding, and next thing you know, I'm a local hero or something."

"Somehow, I think you're downplaying your part in it," Jeannie pressed. "I mean, if you didn't do anything special, why would they be asking you to speak?"

"I guess I just don't see myself as the kind of a leader who would have anything to say about leadership that they haven't already heard. I've been working with a speech coach the past week, and I have some ideas, but it hasn't quite hit me how to organize my thoughts," Marcus admitted.

"I'm sure something will come to you, Marcus."

"Jeannie, there's something I want to talk to you about," Marcus had been waiting for the right time to bring it up, and this was as good a time as any. They had crossed the dam on the lake's south side and were almost half way around.

"O-O-O-K," Jeannie slowed her pace.

"Last time I was here, I saw a picture in Andy's note-book you sketched of me at Lauren's get-together after the dance recital–"

Jeannie interrupted anxiously. "Oh, I hope you weren't offended or embarrassed. I was just taken by a pose, a glimpse, I got of you standing there. I was just hoping to impress Andy, that's all."

"No, no, no, not in the least," Marcus assured her. "The words that come to my mind are impressed and surprised, but not offended. I am amazed at how talented you are. I mean blown away. I had no idea until that moment. It was the expression. Lauren said it looked like

I was searching for something, and I wondered why you saw me that way?"

"But you are. Aren't you?" Jeannie stopped and turned toward Marcus. "Aren't we all searching for something better? Maybe, some more than others. From the first time we met, I could tell you were looking inside yourself for answers to something. You told me then it was how to be a better supervisor. When I met Anna, and we became friends, I could tell you were searching for how she might fit into your future. I guess you're still working on that. Maybe that's what I was seeing. I didn't mean anything by it. Sometimes I see things a certain way and I want to draw them. But it doesn't mean that's the way they really are."

"It's just been on my mind. If you can see it, I wonder who else sees it?" Marcus said.

Jeannie continued, "When I stopped and looked at my little brother again, I saw a twelve-year-old boy, alone and afraid. I realize his continuous, and I mean continuous, pestering was a cry for someone to pay attention to him. I see my mom, who's not getting any younger, petrified of being left alone without any way to survive without a man to take care of her. I guess that's what I love about my drawing. It makes me stop and look at people and wonder about their stories. What do you see, Marcus, when you take time to stop and look at the people you love and who are looking to you for strength and a direction? What are their stories?"

Marcus stood quietly looking into Jeannie's eyes . . . speechless. Then finally, "Where did you come from,

Jeannie Irwin? How did you show up in my life at this time? It's like the wisdom of the sages has been gathered up and poured into this five-foot-six inch, red haired, green-eyed, freckled, eighteen-year old dynamo who just blows me away every time we talk."

Jeannie looked away, "You give me way too much credit. I'm just a kid."

"No, Jeannie, not just a kid. You have a way of making me see and think about things differently."

"Well, . . . " Jeannie paused and tilted her head down shyly to break eye contact. Then, she glanced up without raising her head, "That's what artists do," Jeannie said with a casual smile.

Marcus smiled, holding the gaze in her eyes, "We better keep moving, it looks like we got to talking and forgot to walk," Marcus motioned up the trail.

The conversation took on a lighter tone. Jeannie talked about Andy and Susie. Susie, she knew mostly from their time together at Ms. Rippetoe's dance studio. Jeannie mentioned that she might get to work more with Susie now that she would be a full time instructor. At first, Jeannie would work with an experienced teacher as her assistant, mostly with the younger students.

She spoke of Andy's delight in learning to draw. He, too, had the makings of an artist, she thought. Jeannie mentioned how Andy talked of spending time with his dad at the table, drawing together and telling stories about the picture they were drawing. Then Jeannie abruptly changed the subject as if a thought just leapt into her mind.

"Marcus, do you dance?"

"You're the second girl to ask me that recently. And the answer is, not in a long time," Marcus admitted.

"So, you haven't gone out dancing with Anna?"

"Ummmm. No, we haven't. Usually we go jogging, or do some hiking. We like cycling. We're thinking about joining a cycling club up here. But that's probably on hold, now that she's working more," Marcus sounded disappointed.

"She's working today, I guess."

"Yes. I saw her last night, but won't get to see her again before I go back tomorrow. Then I probably won't see her again until I come up for your graduation. Why do you ask if I dance?"

"It occurred to me that there are some analogies between dancing and leading that might make sense to you. I mean, if you dance," Jeannie offered.

"I've line danced, and like anyone else, I've been to parties and danced."

"I'm talking about something different," Jeannie continued. "Social dancing with a partner."

"You mean like ballroom dancing, cause I don't see myself ever doing that," Marcus raised his palms up in front of himself signaling a halt.

"Not quite. More like a two-step, or a waltz, or swing dancing. You know, where you take a partner in your arms and lead her through the dance," Jeannie explained.

"I've two-stepped some, but I guess I don't understand. What's the connection with leading?" Marcus asked.

"I probably need to show you." Jeannie looked around. They were approaching the park near the community center on the northeast corner of the lake.

"Let's go over there," Jeannie pointed toward the labyrinth that had been donated as a permanent park feature. She took Marcus by the hand and led him to its center.

"I'm going to be the lead, and you are the follower," Jeannie instructed.

"So, I'm the girl, and you're the boy," Marcus teased.

"Something like that," Jeannie chuckled. She grasped Marcus by the shoulders and moved herself squarely in front of him. Taking the lead's position, offset slightly to his right, she held her left hand up and reached her right arm around Marcus, placing her right palm near his shoulder blade. Jeannie instructed Marcus where to place his hands. Then she straightened up and told Marcus to do likewise until he could feel the slight resistance of her holding him. That done, Jeannie just stood in place for several seconds, silent.

"Well?" Marcus finally asked, "What's next?"

"Exactly." Jeannie said. "Point one. Nothing happens until the lead makes the first move." Then Jeannie stepped to her left. Left foot first, then right foot came together. Marcus followed. Then she stepped toward Marcus. He mirrored by stepping back. Then Jeannie moved around stepping and stopping. Marcus followed.

"How do you know what to do, Marcus?" Jeannie asked.

"I could feel where you were going," Marcus answered

"And you were waiting for me to communicate that to you, which means you were doing what all followers do. They wait until the lead shows them the way."

"Elliot, my mentor, told me last week that leaders lead," Marcus pointed out.

"Same thing," Jeannie emphasized. "Now, follow me again," Jeannie instructed.

Jeannie moved, but Marcus did not follow.

"Why didn't you move?" Jeannie asked.

"I couldn't feel anything. I didn't know what to do," Marcus explained.

"That's because I dropped my frame. In other words, I released the resistance between us in my arms and upper body so you couldn't feel the connection. Therefore, you didn't have any way to know what I was going to do. We weren't connected. We weren't communicating," Jeannie explained.

"Even though I was waiting for it," Marcus observed.

"Exactly. You're catching on. Point two. No frame, no connection, no communication," Jeannie said. "Now, you lead."

Jeannie showed Marcus how to hold her in frame as the lead and established the connection between them.

"Now, I'll move however I sense the connection through our frame. I'll even close my eyes so I can't anticipate your lead," Jeannie closed her eyes.

Marcus stepped to the left, but Jeannie stood pat.

"I didn't feel that," Jeannie said opening her eyes. "Try again. This time instead of stepping with your left foot, push off with your right foot causing you to move left.

No
FRAME,
No
CONNECTION,
No
COMMUNICATION

That should keep your feet connected to your arms through your legs and torso."

Jeannie closed her eyes again. Marcus concentrated on pushing with his right foot. Jeannie followed. Marcus soon had the hang of it. After a few missteps, he danced Jeannie around the labyrinth flawlessly.

"There. You've got the idea," Jeannie smiled opening her eyes. "You're leading."

"That really makes sense," Marcus sounded amazed. "What other morsels can you give me?"

"There's the number one leader's rule of social dancing," Jeannie teased.

"And that would be?"

"The number one rule for a leader is show your partner a good time, and keep her safe. After all she usually can't see where she's going. She has to trust that you are thinking of her first and always."

"Damn. This is good stuff," Marcus exclaimed delightedly.

"I'm glad it helps. Maybe someday I can give you some dancing lessons for real," Jeannie offered.

"That would be great," Marcus replied. "Maybe you could teach Anna and me together."

Jeannie dropped her eyes and turned her head toward the lake, "I guess I could." She started toward the edge of the labyrinth, wiping her hands on her hips. "Jeez, it must be getting near noon. We probably need to get back."

Marcus caught up quickly. "Hey, what's the rush?"

Jeannie slowed, letting Marcus fall in step beside her.

Jeannie Irwin's dance leader
advice to Marcus.

"The number one
rule for a leader is
show your partner
a good time, and
keep her safe."

"Listen, I'm going to take Andy and Susie out for a hamburger. Why don't you join us? I'm sure they'd love having you along," Marcus offered.

"I'm supposed to do something with Johnny," Jeannie kept walking looking straight ahead.

"Bring him along, too," it'll give all of us a change to get to know each other better.

"When we get to the house, I'll go in and ask. I'll text you if we can make it," Jeannie agreed.

Jeannie picked up the pace. Marcus matched it. Facebook did not come up again.

Jeannie stopped when the trail reached her yard. She turned to Marcus and hugged him around the neck, "I had fun."

"Me, too," Marcus returned. "Check with Johnny about lunch."

"OK." Jeannie scampered to the back door and went inside without looking back.

Marcus watched until she went inside, then turned back to the trail and jogged the last 200 yards to Lauren's. He reached the bench where Jeannie first met him and sat to catch his breath.

I wonder why Jeannie got so quiet at the last? She hardly said a word the last mile. We were having such a good time at the labyrinth. She really came through with that analogy about dancing and leading. I never thought of it that way. The leader has to take the first step so everyone can move together. Brilliant. I'll use it in the speech. Maybe that's what some of my team means by being decisive.

Marcus's phone buzzed, "next time. sorry." was the extent of Jeannie's message.

Marcus stood up and walked slowly to the veranda. He didn't like the way the walk ended. It didn't feel right. He read Jeannie's text again, then replied, "u sure? I REALLY wanted you to go. please!"

Marcus sat down in his favorite chair on the veranda and looked out toward the still lake surface.

About a minute later, "ok. we'll walk down n 30 min"

Marcus replied, "great. now I'm happy again. c u."

7. On site

Marcus was ready. He rehearsed the speech out loud during his two-hour drive to Grand Lake. He intended to sign in and go to the Wilkes House to get settled, collect his thoughts, and check out the meeting room where his presentation would be the next morning. Marcy gave him specific instructions what to look for and how to familiarize himself with the space so he would be comfortable in it. No surprises.

Now if I can just keep everything in mind Marcy has been telling me the past ten days. I wonder if congressional candidate Eric Greer goes through this kind of prep? OK, Marcus. EGO stuff again. Remember when you first discovered the labyrinth at the lake last October? That self-talk between you and your EGO. This retreat isn't about Eric or Anna or any of that stuff. It's not even about you and all the attention you've been getting at work. The minute you make it all about yourself is the minute you nullify your message. Remember that, Pretty Boy. You know the message is real. You know it because you are living it. You know it because everything you will say is working for you now. That's all you want to say. "Here's my story. Take from it what you will." Don't over analyze this. Just go with it and enjoy the weekend, like the way you ended up enjoying the rehearsal last night even though you were scared to death when you stepped through Marcy's front door.

The dress rehearsal at Marcy's turned out to be a brilliant idea. Marcus had never experienced anything like it. Standing in front of a room full of strangers, the center of complete attention.

Marcy instructed Marcus to arrive an hour before the guests. Reggie was there to make sure Marcus was properly dressed. Marcy had arranged the den, adding several folding chairs, so that there was comfortable seating for twenty. Beverages and an assortment of hors d'oeuvres were available at the bar. Marcus could imagine that this home hosted numerous such gatherings during the years Marcy and Ted entertained. Marcy was in her element.

Marcus had a few minutes to mingle with guests before the speech. Marcy introduced him to an assortment of retired executives, and individuals in the business, education, and non-for-profit communities. She obviously had given some thought to bringing in a diverse group—successful friends from many walks of life and generations.

As he began, Marcus was a little self-conscious, and the butterflies threatened to form. But, just as Marcy had predicted, when he got into his story, and could look into the eyes of the audience, he forgot about himself and became caught up in telling his story.

Afterward, each of the guests congratulated Marcus personally. From what Marcus could see in their eyes, the compliments were sincere, not the kind given out of duty or obligation. It occurred to Marcus, as he mingled, that both Marcy and Teresa were coaxing him into a larger world outside the confines of his project lab and his family circle. Several had asked for his business card, and Marcus was glad Marcy had reminded him to bring an ample supply. It had never crossed his mind that he should.

After the guests left, Marcy debriefed the presentation with him. Everything was positive and affirming. He could tell Marcy was pleased with him, and with herself.

Marcus arrived mid-afternoon at the Phoenix Lodge on the northern shore of Grand Lake. Ten years ago, a consortium of Native American investors had revived the property, which had fallen on difficult economic times in the late '90s. The Johnstone family had given generously to support preserving Oklahoma's Native American heritage. When the Phoenix Lodge opened, Nelson had already committed to being one of its regular corporate customers. The nearby airport could accommodate the corporate aircraft, making the lodge a more attractive corporate destination.

Marcus entrusted his car to valet parking, went inside the lobby and followed the signs directing him to the JEE event. Company executives and guests were already filling the registration area and adjacent lounge. No one looked familiar. Marcus felt suddenly alone.

"Marcus," his name came at him from near the lounge. It was Donovan. "Marcus, glad you're here. I've

What followers expect leaders to tell them:

1. WHERE are we going, and WHY?

2. HOW are we going to get there?

3. Will we be SAFE and OK with you?

4. How will you HELP us?

been keeping an eye out for you." Donovan, apparently engrossed in his official duties from the bulging notebook he carried, extended his right hand. He shook Marcus's hand eagerly, then, putting his arm around Marcus redirected him toward a trio of men huddled to the side. "Marcus, the committee wanted to greet you as soon as you arrived."

He ushered Marcus toward the group, "Hey, everyone," Donovan announced, "look who just drove up." They all stopped their conversation and turned to see Donovan and Marcus coming.

Marcus recognized all three from their meeting last week when Marcus discussed his preliminary presentation ideas with them. His presentation had evolved considerably since then. They looked glad to see him.

"Hi, Marcus, Martin Slater, glad you're here."

"Yes, I remember. Exploration. Thanks."

Jerry Abernathy, HR VP was next, "I hope you'll enjoy your accommodations. Nelson insisted."

"I'm sure I will, Mr. Abernathy. The attention is overwhelming," Marcus admitted. "This is all new to me."

"It's our job to help you feel comfortable. Let us know if there's anything we can do," Jerry said.

"I know we've only met once before, but I feel like I already know you," Jack Ballard, VP of Land Administration, extended a handshake. "I understand you know one of my most popular employees, Teresa Younger."

"Teresa seems to know just about everyone," Marcus smiled.

"She speaks highly of you," Jack added. "We look forward to your presentation in the morning."

"I'm honored that you asked, Mr. Ballard. I'll do my best to live up to your expectations," Marcus said.

Donovan took control, "Excuse us, gentlemen, I need to get Marcus checked in and briefed. We'll see you at dinner." With that Gerald directed Marcus back to the registration table where they got his packet.

"Marcus, I'll introduce you in the morning, and Tony Preston will do the response after your presentation. I want you to look over the intro I've written before you head over to the Wilkes House. I guess you plan to go over there before dinner, right?"

"Yeah, right. I'll just find a quiet corner in the lounge and have something to drink while I look over it. OK?"

"That'll work. I'll find you in ten or fifteen minutes." Donovan excused himself.

Marcus took a seat in a section of the lounge near one of two windows where he could get natural light. A server took his drink order. Marcus read through the introduction.

"I see you're already here." Marcus recognized Erin Morales's voice and glanced up to see her and Elliot Sloan just about to his table. "May we join you?" Erin asked.

Marcus motioned to the two empty chairs.

"Met anyone yet?" Elliot asked.

"Donovan and the rest of the committee when I walked in," Marcus said.

"So, you scored big time, Marcus," Elliot continued. "This is our seventh year here, and even I, a senior VP, have not been invited to stay at the Wilkes House yet?"

"I didn't realize it was that big of a deal," Marcus said.

"Oh, yeah," Elliot emphasized.

"Oh, yeah," Erin echoed simultaneously and nodded, widening her eyes as she spoke.

"Well, Donovan has made me out to be some kind of a super hero in his introduction," Marcus held up the intro. "I'm going to ask him to tone it down quite a bit."

"Gerald has been excited to have you on the program. I know he's just eager to show you off. Millennium has never had a prime slot like this," Erin explained, defending Donovan's enthusiasm.

"I understand, but all the same, I would rather under promise and over deliver instead of the other way around, if you know what I mean," Marcus said.

"Write the intro you want him to give, and I'll talk to him about it," Elliot said.

"I don't want to offend him," Marcus hedged.

"We'll make sure he's OK with it," Erin promised.

Elliot spoke, "Besides, Marcy called me late last night and promised we would be pleased with your speech if you did even half as well as you did at your dress rehearsal."

"I kind of expected to see one or both of you there."

"Marcy invited us, but we talked it over and decided we wanted to wait and hear it for the first time in the morning," Erin admitted.

Johnstone Energy Enterprises
"ReEnergizing America's Future"

Executive team:

Corporate:
Nelson Johnstone, Chairman & CEO
Randall Allenbaugh, CFO
Wallace (Wally) Pierce, Chief of Strategic Development
Tom Hayes, Sr. Legal Counsel
Alycia Chen, Chief IT Officer
Beverly Trudeau, Director Corporate Relations

Johnstone Oil & Gas
Cody Watkins, President & COO
Aaron Jackson, VP Drilling
Elliot Sloan, VP Production
Jack Ballard, VP Land
Tom Best, VP Marketing
Martin Slater, VP Exploration
Bill Sanders, VP Finance
Jerry Abernathy, VP Human Resources
Sandra Grossman, Legal Counsel

Millennium Energy
Anthony (Tony) Preston, President & COO
Selena Glenn, VP Administration
Gerald Donovan, VP Research & Development
Beth Johnston, VP Finance
Thad Bergstrom, VP Wind Division
Bryan Meyer, VP Solar Division

"I look around, and I don't see many familiar faces. For the most part, I see some of these people at the annual holiday banquet, but I've never met them," Marcus said.

"Yeah, even in corporate-wide events, everyone tends to hang out with their own kind," Erin observed. "A birds-of-a-feather thing, you know."

"I hear you've been having lunch with Teresa Younger and her friends," Elliot added, turning to Marcus.

"That fact seems to be getting around," Marcus chuckled.

"People like Teresa and Marcy make great allies. They will get you into groups easier than you can on your own," Elliot offered. "They are connectors. Events like this one are opportunities to grow connections. Gerald, Erin, Tony, and I will stay close and help you meet people. I think you're going to have a great weekend, Marcus. We're excited to see you here," Elliot encouraged.

"Marcus, you have blossomed over the last six months," Erin beamed. "I know sometimes you get frustrated, but you have handled some tough situations well. You've certainly been responsive to my coaching. The thing that pleases me most is that you ask for my help."

"That's because you've been a great supervisor to me," Marcus returned the compliment.

Donovan returned, "Had a chance to look over that intro?"

Marcus begged of, "Got involved talking to Erin and Elliot. How about I take it over to the Wilkes House, and I'll give it back at dinner?"

"That'll work," Donovan agreed. "If you'll excuse me. Official business."

*   *   *

The point on which the Victorian Wilkes House sits, jutted into the Grand Lake o'the Cherokees so that the view from the third floor master bedroom suite provided an unobstructed panorama of the lake, panning a full 225 degrees. The only major alterations to the property were the meeting space, necessary commercial kitchen, and parking. The landscaping disguised the sizable parking area just inside the entrance gates so that boaters would only see green space.

A valet, stationed at the front steps of the home, greeted Marcus as he pulled into the circle driveway. The valet instructed Marcus that he would attend to the luggage and park his car.

A hostess welcomed Marcus at the front door and escorted him to his room on the second floor. She informed Marcus that the Wilkes House guests would be assembling in the main floor parlor for cocktails at 5:00 p.m. Cars would be provided to take the party to the lodge for the banquet.

Marcus asked if he could see the meeting space. The hostess gave Marcus directions to the meeting room and told him, Ramos, the meeting coordinator, would be in that area until 5:30. Marcus would be welcome there any time.

So this is what first class looks like, Marcus thought as he took a moment to look around the room. *I cannot believe that I am standing right here, right now, getting ready to have before-dinner drinks with the executives of this company. If Anna could see me now. Better yet, if she could be here with me.*

A knock at the door. The valet brought in Marcus's luggage and car keys, but offered to keep the keys should he choose. There would be someone on duty over night, should any guest require assistance. Marcus offered a tip, but the valet refused. Gratuities from guests were not necessary.

Marcus decided he should relax before showering and dressing for dinner. He had to rewrite his intro for Donovan. A restored Victorian sideboard with leaded glass doors caught Marcus's eye. On it sat a dish of assorted fruit and glass bowls of raw nuts: almonds, cashews, and pistachios. And beside them, an electric teakettle with an assortment of herbal teas, and six bottles of spring water.

Marcus brewed a cup of tea, kicked off his shoes, opened an outside door to the second story porch that wrapped around three sides of the house, and retreated to the sofa in the seating area. Definitely first class.

* * *

Marcus could hear multiple conversations mingling together as he entered the corridor from the meeting wing to the main parlor. Ramos had graciously walked Marcus through the mechanics of the room. He even wired Marcus with the clip-on mic he would use in the morning and did a quick sound check. Marcus had never used one before, and Ramos had a few pointers on how the mic would best work for him.

Nelson was the first to see Marcus coming into the parlor and hurried to greet him, hand extended, "Marcus. Come join us. I was wondering if you were going to make it downstairs."

"Sorry to come in a little late, but I went to check out the meeting room. It took a few minutes longer than I expected," Marcus apologized, reaching out to accept Nelson's hand.

"Let me introduce you around," Nelson offered. "Everyone, everyone, may I have your attention." The room settled, "I want to present Marcus Winn, the young engineer from Millennium who will be speaking in the morning about his experiences as a new team leader. Please, make him feel welcome."

Then Nelson accompanied him to each cluster of guests as they introduced themselves. Tony Preston, Millennium's COO, was the only other executive Marcus knew by sight. Marcus noticed that he was by far the youngest person in the room. The next youngest would be Nelson's daughter, Lizzy and her husband Travis, both early forties. The two other special guests, Marcus learned, would be Jackson DeLaney, a former professional football coach turned motivational speaker, and the U.S. Congressman representing Tulsa, Steven Wakefield. They would arrive tomorrow.

"Thank you for your hospitality and for inviting me to stay at the Wilkes House," Marcus told Nelson and his wife, Patty.

"Did you find everything agreeable in your room?" Patty asked.

"Yes, ma'am. You don't usually find an electric teakettle in hotels. I took immediate advantage of it."

"Well, you have Mavis Harvey to thank for that," Patty confessed. "When she heard you were staying here, she let us know you only drank herbal teas."

"She's a gem. I see her several mornings a week at the Black Gold Café. I think she's become an institution in her own way in the company," Marcus said.

"Mavis is like family to us," Nelson added. "And she's a big fan of yours, too."

Marcus blushed.

Wally Pierce and Tony Preston joined the group. Wally spoke. "Marcus, I was just telling Tony that you've got some talent on your team. They really impressed me with your Burns Flat presentation. Especially that young man, Sanjar. Obviously, he thoroughly researched our company history."

"Sanjar has a way of keeping things light and positive. We can count on him to keep us entertained," Marcus acknowledged the compliment.

Tony jumped in, "I was impressed that your entire team wanted to show its support for the presenters by being in the room. That's the kind of teamwork we'd like to see more of."

Wally added, "Your team got it. You reminded us of the entrepreneurial spirit that built this company. We don't want to lose that, and we hope you'll be able to convey that spirit to our leaders tomorrow."

"I'll do my best," Marcus smiled, all the while thinking, *But I'm not a miracle worker.*

* * *

Oklahoma's May weather can be volatile and locally vio-
lent. From his vantage point on the deck outside his
room, Marcus could see the electrified tops of thunder-
heads to the southeast putting on a light show. The
northern most edge of the weather system had passed
over the lake as the dinner was ending around 8:00 p.m.
By the time they had left the lodge to return to the
Wilkes House, the line of showers had passed. The air
smelled fresh. No tornadoes had come from any of the
cells.

The informal dinner had been uneventful. Thankfully. Nelson's welcoming comments were brief. Marcus
ended up at a table with Tony, and other Millennium attendees.

Marcus shared a limo with Tony Preston, Randall
Allenbaugh, and their wives. That gave Tony his chance
to encourage Marcus during the ride over. He also
praised Erin Morales for her leadership. He confess that
if he ever lost Thad Bergstrom as vice president of the
wind division, Erin was ready to step in without any drop
in effectiveness.

"Our day is coming, Marcus. Our day is coming, and
you are in on the ground floor," Tony's eyes danced as he
spoke.

"But you know, Tony, Millennium will eventually
have to carry its own weight, revenue wise," Allenbaugh

On site   109

reminded. "It can't continue to be Nelson's hobby, my friend."

"Of course, Randall," Tony replied. "Spoken like a true CFO, as it should be. We're so close, and I'm banking on our talent pool, like young Marcus here, to make it happen sooner than later," Tony affirmed. "Right, Marcus?"

"Yes sir, Mr. Preston. The Burns Flat field has been steadily improving efficiency. The team is committed," Marcus affirmed.

That's what it came down to, Marcus reflected. Dollars and cents. ROI. He knew Allenbaugh was right. And Jim Bob Danner's opinion that Nelson was wasting his resources with Millennium had to be widespread among the oil and gas executives.

Millennium's delegation represented only about ten percent of the audience Marcus would face in about twelve hours. How much credibility could he expect to have in front of that group? It wasn't an audience hand picked by Marcy.

Marcus's phone buzzed. It was still on silent. Marcy was calling.

"Well, how did you know I was just thinking about you?" Marcus answered the call.

"Thought I would check in. Did you do everything I suggested, looking at the meeting room and all?" Marcy asked.

"I'm set there. Even did a mic check."

"Good. How's everything else going?"

"I'm being treated like a celebrity. It's a little overwhelming. First class all the way."

"Nervous?"

"Some. I know I'm not here to justify Millennium, but that's the feeling I keep getting. Like the future of the company is riding on this speech," Marcus admitted.

"Stay focused on your story like we rehearsed. All that other stuff is a distraction. You can't control that in the morning anyway," Marcy reminded him.

"I hear you, but it's a lot to have on my mind," Marcus admitted.

"Marcus, remember, your message is just as relevant to oil and gas as it is to Millennium. Your story resonated with everyone at your rehearsal last night. A couple of them want their managers to hear what you had to say. Just focus on the message. Some people will think it's great; others might not. It's not as important that everyone agree as it is how passionate you are about it," Marcy said.

"I hear you."

"Do you believe in what you are saying?" Marcy asked.

"Yes. Absolutely."

"Then, you'll be just fine," Marcy affirmed. "Trust me. Be yourself, and you'll be OK." Marcy paused. "OK?"

"OK," Marcus agreed. "Thanks for the encouragement."

"I'm proud of you. Now get a good night's sleep."

"Will do," and with that Marcus ended the call.

8. Center stage

Marcus stepped off the front porch of the Wilkes House and went through his pre-jogging stretching routine. A short run in the fresh morning air would prep him physically and mentally for the big day. He headed up the driveway, out the entrance gates, and down the winding lane past the lakeside estates that populated either side of the lane. It was one mile to the intersection of the main county road. The up and back should do the trick and still give him plenty of time to dress for the day and get to the family-style breakfast by 7:00 a.m. in the main dining room.

Marcus returned to his room to find his phone lit up with messages. He uncapped a bottle of water and stepped out onto the deck to read through them.

First from Anna, "good luck today. you'll do great."

He replied, "thx. talk tonight late?"

Next from Jeannie, "break a leg. want to hear all about it."

Marcus answered, "thanks. ur dancing lesson helped. will explain later."

What's this? One from Dad? Since when does Dad text? "Proud of you son. Good luck. Mom sends love."

Marcus tapped in his answer, "thanks for everything dad. love you both."

Marcus swallowed the last of the water, drew in one more deep breath of lake air, and went inside. He was ready.

* * *

The opening session would begin at 9:00 a.m. The transformation from quiet executive retreat to corporate meeting facility started shortly after 8:00 a.m. at the Wilkes House. The parking lot populated with luxury autos and SUVs with early arrivers getting the choice places closest to the front door. An assortment of beverages, fruit, and pastries were positioned in the spacious parlor and the foyer of the meeting facility. Conversations were subdued, but as more attendees arrived, the individual conversations became lost in the cacophony.

Marcus intended to maintain a low profile, but Donovan found him early. "Marcus, about the introduction. Elliot discussed it with me last night during dinner. Are you sure this is all you want me to say?"

"If you please. I think less is more, in my case. Gerald, the intro you wrote was flattering, and I appreciate that you want to build me up to this group. I would just feel more comfortable keeping the intro to the basics. Besides, a more complete bio is in the program anyway," Marcus explained.

"Sure. I see what you mean. Maybe I did go overboard a little. It's just that —"

Marcus interrupted, "I know. I know this is a big chance for Millennium to shine. I'll do my best to give you reason to brag. OK? If I live up to your billing, then you can lay it on thick."

"Deal," Donovan smiled and patted Marcus on the shoulder and excused himself to get back to his hosting duties.

Marcus felt his phone vibrate. Dan Packwood sent a message, "Hey, boss. Team sends best wishes. You'll be great. Will this be on video?"

Marcus replied, "thx. probably, but I'll check."

Sure enough. Ramos confirmed that all sessions are recorded and given to the client. Then he told Marcus the camera was just another attendee and would not distract him.

Reggie had anticipated the video when he suggested Marcus's wardrobe for the presentation: a navy blue, two-button gabardine suit tailored to Marcus's athletic build, with unpleated trousers and a solid sky blue French cuff dress shirt worn open collar. According to Reggie, navy blue projects trustworthiness, leadership, and authority, and sky blue is open, friendly, and exhilarating. Marcus was comfortable in his clothes, and his skin.

Millennium employees had captured seats on the third and forth rows. At least he knew where to look for friendly faces. He took a seat in the back for the first session.

Cody Watkins, JE Oil & Gas COO, was first up. He gave an update of company performance and projections. Standard stuff. Then he addressed some new technology they had been developing to improve well performance and introduced Elliot, the vice president of production, to fill in the details. This was the first time Marcus had heard Elliot talk about his own work. Marcus found himself intrigued. Not only did Elliot impress him, Marcus found himself proud to be Elliot's mentoring protégé–and by association, connected to every other person in that room. As a group, just as Elliot had told him before, they were not his enemy. Marcus relaxed.

During the break, Marcus moved to the front of the room where Ramos fixed the mic and had Marcus do a brief sound check. Everyone in the Millennium delegation offered support and encouragement. Marcus caught himself looking around the room to locate the video cameras, then resolved not to look at them.

Before settling into his front row seat, Marcus scanned the crowd as it refilled for his session. He counted ten women–five were from the Millennium delegation, then there was Patty Johnstone sitting with Nelson about two-thirds of the way back stage left. Lizzy sat on Patty's left. He spotted Beverly Trudeau from corporate relations speaking with Ramos. That's eight. He did not know the other two women. Elliot was one of three African-Americans.

Again, Marcus appeared to be one of the youngest in the room–perhaps the youngest. For the first time Marcus realized that the diversity represented among his Burns Flat project team was not reflected in the leadership of Johnstone Energy as a whole. Interesting, since he had seen more women in the corporate cafeteria and throughout the campus. Marcus wondered about the prospects for smart, assertive women like Teresa Younger to move up into management at Johnstone. He smiled as the image of Teresa sitting across the café table calling him, "Buzz," flashed through his mind. He looked forward to seeing her Monday morning. His phone vibrated. *Who could that be?* He started not to look, but did.

"Pulling for you Buzz. kick ass." Teresa had a way with words.

Her timing was impeccable. It was 10:29.

Marcus was pumped. The same feeling he remembered getting before a big cross-country race in college.

Gerald Donovan stepped on the platform at the front of the room holding a wireless mic. The room quieted as Donovan waited.

"I'm Gerald Donovan, vice president of research and development for Millennium Energy. I have the special honor this morning of introducing our featured speaker,"

OK, Donovan, don't go off script. Low key, remember.

"There's a lot I could say about this young man . . ."

Back to the script, Gerald. Back to the script.

"But I'll let him speak for himself. His official bio is in your program. He came to Millennium fresh out of college at Oklahoma State. He is currently the team leader for the Burns Flat wind farm project. He impressed me several months ago with his ideas about supervising and leading, and I asked him to present them here today. From the size of the crowd, and the fact that I see several spouses attending this session, you are as curious as I am to hear what he has to say. It's my pleasure to present one of our own, Marcus Winn."

Donovan started the applause, which was polite, but died out quickly as Marcus took the platform.

Marcus walked to the center of the platform, placed his notes on the lectern, dropped his arms to his side, straightened his spine, shoulders back, standing tall, panned the audience smiling . . . and began.

"You might be wondering why I'm standing in front of you this morning, in this prime time slot, to talk to you about leadership. I've been wondering the same thing for several weeks.

[subdued scattered laughter]

"You might think it's because the team I supervise, the Burns Flat wind farm project, recently defended our funding before the corporate council, and also secured funding for all wind projects going forward. That got a lot of attention. I've been told there's been a buzz about it.

[More subdued scattered laughter]

"But you would be wrong.

"I was invited to speak today because I was on the verge of failing as a new supervisor, and was told so in October.

[Pause, room is dead silent. Marcus took three steps to stage right, the audience's left, then turned back and glanced at Erin Morales sitting on the third row center aisle seat.]

"Erin Morales, my supervisor, tried to help me see my challenges, but I was too proud to hear it. I insulted her out of that pride and denial.

[Marcus looked back into the audience.]

"Wisely, she sent me home early that day and told me to take the weekend to reflect on what she had said. It turned out to be a moment of truth for me.

"I drove in anger to my sister's lake home near Springfield. I intended to call my dad and complain to him how unfairly I was being treated. I wanted someone to be on my side, and tell me I was right, and that everyone would come around when they truly saw my brilliance.

[Some scattered laughter.]

"I wanted to say to him, How dare they not understand how hard I work?

"How dare they not appreciate my standards of performance?

"How dare they not recognize how I urge my team to go the extra mile, to excel, to sacrifice?

"How dare they not understand that I only insisted on all the same things I was taught about performing, and striving for excellence, and having a winning mindset.?

"How dare they?

[Marcus paused returned to center state dropping his eyes as he walked.]

"But I decided not to make that call. My Ego would not let me see the truth.

[Marcus looked back to the audience making eye contact with a single person in the second row stage right. Someone not in the Millennium section.]

"I did not know what to do next, or who to turn to.

[Marcus paused, and scanned the faces in the audience. They were waiting. He had them.

Marcus walked two paces to stage left, the audience's right.]

"It turned out to be an eye-opening weekend. I met several people, some of them for the first time, who, although unaware of my crisis, gave me a whole new way to see myself and to understand my role as a new supervisor. Not one of them had any clue that what they showed me would change everything for me . . . and save my job.

"I returned to work with a written plan to improve. Erin gave me ninety days to turn it around, and she set me up with Elliot Sloan, who graciously agreed to be a mentor, and to help me keep my head on straight.

"Gerald Donovan sat in on my ninety-day review. At the conclusion of that review, he asked me if I would be willing to share what I learned and what I did at this retreat. I agreed. And that's the story of why I am here today.

"But my speech is about the rest of the story–what became my new way to lead.

[Marcus returned to center stage.]

"In the limited time we have this morning, if I could leave you with just one thought, it would be this. That I believe it's my responsibility as a team leader to create an environment where every member feels they can unleash the creative energy of their personal INPowerment.

"I call it IN-powerment, spelled, I-N powerment, because the energy comes from within the person. As a leader, the best I can do is make it possible for those I lead to find their own way to be successful. I am an enabler to those who will be IN-powered. I must trust in that motivational force they already possess.

"I believe this because of six principles of leading I learned from three people in particular that weekend when Erin sent me off to think about my attitude, and my future.

"In the next few minutes, I want to share those with you:

- *one thing I learned from my nine-year-old nephew,*

- *two things I learned from my sister and brother-in-law, and*
- *three things I learned from a red-haired, teen-age girl I came across, sobbing beside the lake when I went out for a walk.*

"When I arrived, my nephew, Andy, was excited about me going to watch him play soccer Saturday morning. That surprised me because by the end of soccer season last year, Andy had decided to never play on the soccer team again. Why? He had a coach who yelled and screamed at the boys to play harder, keep their head in the game, and to stop making him look bad as a coach. He hollered, 'Don't you want to win?'

"Andy told me the hollering did not help. Everyone already wanted to win. . . . always.

"What changed? Andy got a different coach. This coach taught the boys how to play the game and how much fun it was. She simply challenged the boys to practice the skills; that pride came from giving their honest best effort; and that learn-

ing to play as a team gave them the best chance to win.

"As Andy told me, 'She made it fun again.'

"And they did their share of winning.

"That's right. Andy's coach was a young woman who volunteered at the last minute to coach when, thankfully, the previous coach was told he would not be coaching in the league any longer.

"When I told Andy I was surprised his coach was a girl, he gave me a puzzled look and asked, 'What difference does that make, if she's good at it?'

[laughter. The women applauded.]

"But what I learned from Andy, is that everyone is already motivated to win. No one has to convince us that winning is a good thing. I realized that everyone on my team came to work every day wanting to do a good job at something they enjoyed, and to feel good about their accomplishments.

"If I helped make that happen for them, I would also look good as a supervisor.

[Widespread applause.]

"We can learn a lot from our children . . . if we are paying attention.

[Laughter and applause.]

"By the way, how many of you have children?

[Marcus raised his hand as he asked. Most in the audience raised a hand.]

"That brings me to two things I learned from my sister and brother-in-law.

"I love going to the home that they have created on the shore of a private community lake. It's like a resort to me.

"When they bought it as newlyweds, it was run down, and an eyesore. Everyone warned them that it was way more house than they needed.

But they were so clear minded about their vision. They saw the potential in it. Over the years they reclaimed it, and built a special place. Lauren told me she and Jarod talked almost daily about the kind of home they wanted to create together.

"Everyone is already MOTIVATED to win.
No one has to convince us that winning is a good thing.
Everyone on my team came to work every day wanting to do a good job at something they enjoyed, and to feel good about their accomplishments."

As Jarod and I sat under the veranda on that trip, he told me it was just as he imagined it would be someday when he first saw the property.

"Jarod gazed out on his handiwork, because he built most of it himself, and he explained it didn't come all at once. They built it together from a common vision of what could be.

"Family and friends saw only a dilapidated house on a neglected lot that was too much to take on. Lauren and Jarod saw a home filled with family, laughter, and joy.

"The first thing I learned from Lauren and Jarod was the importance of being clear minded: having a clear vision that produces clarity of purpose and action. Every incremental step moved them closer to the grand vision they began with.

"They taught me that an INPowering leader is clear minded.

"I have a vision for what I believe the Burns Flat wind farm can become. That's what we talked about when we explained why funding should continue.

"Wind energy is hard. The odds might even be against us. But the oil patch that became Tulsa, that, in turn, gave rise to Johnstone Oil and Gas, was hard, and unpredictable, and frustrating, and at times dangerous. Yet, here we are today. . .

[Marcus extended both arms wide outward, palms up, and pivoted from the waist, panning the room from the audience's left to right as he delivered the last line.]

. . . the realization of a vision, a dream, a passion—one of the most successful independents in the world that took three generations to build. It didn't happen all at once.

[Loud applause began before Marcus finished his phrase. His volume rose to speak over the applause. Some stood in ovation. He had to wait several seconds for the applause to quiet. Then he continued in a much more subdued tone and volume.]

"We talked a lot about family that weekend. Lauren and Jarod talked about how being a parent is not a job, . . . it's a lifestyle.

"Think how your life fundamentally changed when your first child was born. Until that time, you were mostly concerned about yourself. You and

your spouse probably did kind of as you pleased, when you pleased. Right?

> [Everyone was nodding. Marcus noticed several couples in the audience glanced at each other as if to say, "Remember those days?"]

"Then along came your child, and it stopped being about you. Everything was about caring for your baby, and growing your family.

"It's the parent's responsibility to create a family environment, a culture, where everyone is safe, and happy, and able to grow.

"It occurred to me how much I love being in their home, and how good I feel in that space, and that I never look forward to leaving. But, as I learned that weekend, not all parents put their children first, and not every home is happy and wholesome the way Lauren's and Jarod's is.

"So, the second thing I learned from them is that when I became a supervisor, my work life fundamentally changed. Only I didn't recognize that fact at the time. You see, when I became a supervisor, it wasn't about just me any longer. Supervising, managing, and leading is not a job. It's

a life style: 24-7-365. Even today, here we are at this lovely resort, but how many of you are thinking about how things are going back at the office?

[Much laughter and heads nodding.]

"We never get away from it. Do we?"

"As a supervisor, I am responsible for the care and feeding, so-to-speak, of those who have been entrusted to me. Just like you want your children to trust you with their lives, so also our employees look to us, trusting that their wellbeing is first and foremost on our mind.

"I learned that an INPowering leader is people oriented.

"My personal moment of truth was realizing that I had not made the transition from ME to WE, that I had been neglecting the well being of my team. If I did not make the change from E-go to We-go immediately, I would surely fail as a new leader.

[Marcus paused, broke eye contact with the audience, moved back to center stage, and re-established eye contact with one of the participants sitting about half way back on the center isle.]

"Now, about the red-haired teenager I came across sitting beside the lake, sobbing.

"I could tell she was distraught, even though she tried to hide it. I did not know whether to keep walking, or to stop and try to help. As it turned out, I ended up sitting quietly beside her near the water's edge.

"I waited for her to speak.

"Eventually, she confessed that she wanted to run away from home because her mother and step-dad ignored her and showed no interest in, or support for her activities–her life. Jeannie felt she was not wanted, but was trapped.

"She told me that when she turned eighteen in a month, she intended to be out of there. She described her situation briefly. When I met her mother and step-dad, I could see why she was distraught.

"Contrasting Jeannie's family environment with that of my sister's home hit me like a punch in the gut, as I thought about my own actions toward my team members. I wondered, just as Jeannie wanted to get away from her mom and step-dad, did my own team want to get away from me because of the way I had treated, or I should say, mis-treated them?

"Erin told me she was concerned that some team members were looking elsewhere for support instead of to me. I feared she was right, but was insulted that she was accusing me of being a 'bad parent,' so-to-speak.

"The first thing Jeannie taught me was that every person matters. We all have hopes, dreams, expectations, and disappointments. Every person is inherently valuable, without exception. And that everything is personal . . . everything . . . always.

"All that matters to each and every one of us is the quality of our lives. We are just trying how to figure it all out.

"Furthermore, we are all connected in a network of relationships, and I am personally responsible and accountable for the quality of my relationships . . . just as you are for yours.

"As a supervisor, and a leader, I must be people-oriented before I can earn the trust of my followers. They will know if I don't care.

[Marcus glanced out over a silent audience. All eyes were on him.]

"The other two things I learned from Jeannie, I learned last Saturday, as I was putting the finishing touches on this presentation.

"Jeannie is a talented dancer. She takes lessons in the same dance studio as my twelve-year old niece; so, I've seen Jeannie perform. Next month, after graduation, Jeannie will become a full time assistant instructor in that studio to help pay for her college. She decided not to run away.

"She taught me that leaders lead. She explained it saying when couples dance together . . .

[Marcus approximated what it looked like to be in a dance frame. He pretended to be holding a partner. He stood motionless, then took a step forward with his left foot on cue with the next phrase.]

" . . . the dance cannot begin until the leader makes the first move—takes the first step.

"I remember delivering the news to my team that our funding was in jeopardy and we had to come up with a presentation to explain why it should be continued. I can still see the stunned expressions. Everyone looked at me as if to say, 'OK, what do we do now? What's the first move?'

"In a sense, I had to take the first step so we could all move together.

"Think about it. When in doubt or crisis, and people don't know what to do next what will they do? They will turn and look at someone in the group and ask, 'OK, what do we do now?' The person they look to is the leader. It might or might not be the supervisor–the official leader by title.

"A leader is someone who can help us go places we cannot go on our own, either because we don't know how, or we are afraid. Followers will look to someone they trust and believe in. Followers need their leaders to answer four crucial questions for them:

First . . .Where are we going, and why?

Second . . . How are we going to get there?

Third . . . Will we be OK? Are we safe with you?

and Fourth . . . How will you help us make it?

[Marcus paused to reflect, and found himself going off script to add a comment that came to him in the moment.]

"I believe those questions apply in every size and type of business, at every level of government, in our religious institutions, throughout the community, and in every family.

[Solid applause across the audience. Marcus resumed his speech as prepared.]

"Jeannie demonstrated that leaders lead. They step up, because sitting it out is not an option . . . if you want to dance . . . It's your choice.

"Jeannie's third lesson is connected to the second one. Leaders create a frame, a structure, and a safe space in which the dance is communicated and carried out.

"This dance frame does several things. It establishes a way to communicate through mutual connection. The dancers respond to each other's give-and-take. If that frame is lost, communication

"A LEADER is someone who can help us go places we cannot go on our own, either because we don't know how, or we are afraid."

fails, and the dance falls apart until the frame is re-established.

"This is so simple and basic, that it's profound. Connection is communication. Structure is safety and boundary. Yet, dancers can still express a measure of individual style within it.

"As a leader it's up to me to establish a frame-work, a space, where my team can safely communicate openly and honestly about what's going on. This creative tension is a healthy interaction that allows a free exchange of information to make our work together successful. Otherwise, everything is at risk of falling apart.

"It's a two-way communication in which I, as leader, am a willing participant. I must be present and connected. Everyone must know they can tell the truth, as they understand it, without the risk of reprisal or ridicule.

"One of my team put me to the test last week. She had suggested we do a lessons learned de-briefing of the team presentation project. The team agreed.

"When it came time to have that debriefing, she asked me if she could facilitate it as a learning experience for her. She explained that if she were to improve her chances of moving up, she needed to develop that skill.

"In my old way of leading, I would have insisted on running that meeting because, as the supervisor, it was my job to be in control. This time, however, in my new way of leading, I agreed. I let her take the lead, and I had to learn to follow. She was splendid. I hope her initiative will encourage others to ask for similar opportunities.

"One of my personal lessons learned during the presentation project, is how much more talent there is on the team that I had not seen before. Each did the part they were responsible for, but they stepped up offering to help each other, drawing on talents and interests they did not typically get to use on the job.

"All I did was try to create an environment where they could do their best and support it. I did

not have to make them want to win, I just had to allow them the room to win.

"I learned that an INPowering leader is performance driven, not as a task master, but as a trusted leader of talented individuals who want to perform and succeed.

"To summarize:

"Leading is a life style,

"Leaders lead intentionally,

"Leaders provide a clear vision of what can be and why it matters,

"Leaders provide a safe structure where two-way communication leads to an environment of trust,

"Because everyone is naturally motivated to win, to do the best they know how, at something they enjoy, to be proud of their effort,

"Because everyone has a story, and everyone matters, without exception.

"Being people oriented, clear minded, and performance driven helps me keep it all in balance in my new way to lead.

"I go back to where I began. It's my responsibility as a team leader to create an environment where every member feels they can unleash the creative energy of their personal INPowerment.

"I asked Lauren and Jarod, 'Do the kids ever disobey?'

"Yes.

"Do they ever fight?

"Like cats and dogs.

"Do they ever disappoint you?

"Sometimes.

"Do they ever make you mad?

"Regularly. All of the above. Then, they turn around and make you so proud you think you'll just pop.

> [Marcus could see heads nodding and wide-spread smiles. Couples looked at each other. Marcus could see that Nelson sat with his arm around Patty's shoulder.]

"I'm so proud of my team and what they have accomplished.

"Will we win in the end? I believe we will. It's early in the game. Regardless, I promise you, we *will put every ounce of creative energy into our effort . . . And we will have a blast.*

"I'm so proud of my team I could just pop. I'm proud to be part of Millennium Energy, and I'm proud to be your partner in ReEnergizing America's Future with Johnstone Energy Enterprises.

"I look forward to meeting more of you this weekend.

"Thank you."

To Marcus's left, the Millennium delegation leapt to their feet in ovation. Marcus noticed Nelson, Patty, and Lizzy stand almost as quickly. Around the room, others began to rise. Some had glanced toward Nelson first, then followed his lead. Marcus looked for Elliot, who had sat about six rows back, stage right. He was on his feet, beaming and clapping enthusiastically. Marcus caught Elliot's eye, and Elliot acknowledged with an approving nod and wink.

Marcus stood at center stage soaking up the applause, unprepared for how he should respond. Part of him wanted to get off the stage as quickly as possible; the other part wanted the applause to last forever. It was addictive.

Thankfully, Tony Preston was standing at the corner of the riser, waiting for the appropriate moment to ascend the stage for his response. At the first sign the ovation began to wane, he stepped up and walked toward Marcus, extending his right hand. Tony turned Marcus toward the audience and put his arm around Marcus's shoulder. The applause died, and everyone sat.

Tony spoke, keeping his hold on Marcus while looking him in the eyes, "Marcus, thank you for sharing your journey with us and for reminding us that we are all part of one excellent company with a common mission. And right now, I'm so proud of you that I could just pop."

Then Tony looked back toward the audience, "Marcus has set a high standard for us this weekend, hasn't he? Let's hear it one more time for Marcus Winn."

Applause again filled the room, the loudest from the Millennium rows. Marcus took the cue and left the stage. Gerald Donovan, obviously overjoyed, embraced Marcus as soon as he stepped off the stage.

Nelson had walked up from his seat to shake Marcus's hand. He leaned to speak into Marcus's ear, "Great job, Marcus. Hell of a speech. We'll find time to talk later."

"Thank you. I look forward to it, sir," Marcus acknowledged.

Nelson returned to his seat next to Patty. Donovan and Marcus retook their seats on the front row. Marcus felt like he could finally relax and enjoy the rest of the weekend. He breathed deeply, closed his eyes, bowed his head, and exhaled as he let all the pent up energy dissipate.

Tony Preston began with his response, but Marcus was lost in his own thoughts and the emotional rush that had swallowed him whole.

MARCUS! YOU WERE FREAKIN' AWESOME! I might be hooked on speaking. This is like no high I ever felt in my days of competitive cross-country running. Being totally in that zone . . . that connection between the audience and me . . . everyone riveted on my story . . . then the applause. Everything Marcy taught me was right on. She's worth every dollar I'm paying her. . . Wait, she's never said anything about being paid. Surely, she expects me to pay. I hope she didn't assume I expected her help for free.

I wish Anna had been here to experience this with me. Take that, all-eyes-in-the-room-on-you, Eric Greer. You're not the only one who can deliver a story!! Yes! Marcus! You killed!

I could use a vacation after this. Man, the last seven or eight months have been a hell of a roller coaster. At last, I feel like I have some breathing room. It would be nice to drive into the mountains and get some fresh air. Maybe I can make that happen.

Wonder if I can get a copy of the video? Would like my family to see it. I bet they would have never thought Little Markie could pull off something like this—not in a million years.

Donovan stood, breaking Marcus's mental side trip. Time for the Q & A. Jerry Abernathy and Tom Best, VP of Marketing, would field questions, along with Marcus. *Hope the Jim Bobs go easy on me,* Marcus thought.

"A New Way to Lead"
Six themes of Marcus's speech

1. *Everyone is already motivated to win.*

2. *Clarity of vision produces clarity of purpose and action.*

3. *It's the leader's job to provide a safe place where team members can grow.*

4. *Every person is inherently valuable, without exception.*

5. *Leaders lead. The team is looking for the leader to take the first step.*

6. *The leader sets the boundaries for quality two-way communication.*

9. Afterglow

Marcus strolled along the shoreline toward the tip of the point about a hundred yards from the Wilkes House. He was still coming down from the exhilaration of the day's events. A southerly breeze crossing the lake refreshed Marcus as he paused and faced toward the open waters. Waves hit the shores with a gentle rhythm. A hint of distant honeysuckle perfumed the air.

Thankfully, no Jim Bobs had shown up. There had been more questions about how Marcus came up with his leadership ideas. Questions about how to balance performance with being people oriented surfaced mostly.

One comment did test Marcus momentarily. Marcus only caught the first name, Pete, who said with some certainty, "I just don't think most people will perform unless they know they are being watched and held accountable. I believe in tough love, with a dose of the brutal truth. That keeps them on their toes from my experience."

Marcus tried to respond without being argumentative, "I certainly agree that being performance driven and accountable are important, and negative reinforcement is sometimes necessary. I believe that positive motivation toward clear objectives is more powerful; like benefiting from a tail wind instead of fighting a head wind." The response seemed to be well received.

On the whole, the Q & A was cordial. Marcus thought it was good experience for thinking on his feet.

Marcy agreed, when he called her during lunch to report that his presentation went even better than expected. But she had already seen a video clip of it Elliot had sent on his cell phone. She wanted to have him over soon to review the full video when it was available. Beverly Trudeau had already promised to send her a copy.

NFL coach Jackson DeLaney spoke at the evening banquet at the Phoenix Lodge. He was more from the tough love school of motivation. But, hey, how do you argue with three Super Bowl rings and a spot in the hall of fame?

One point that DeLaney agreed with Marcus about, however, is the need for clarity–clarity of vision and expectations . . . and, of course, teamwork. Everyone talks about teamwork.

DeLaney told more jokes than Marcus did, and DeLaney's standing ovation lasted about twice a long, but who's counting. Everyone wanted their picture taken with DeLaney, even Marcus. So far, no one had requested having their picture taken with Marcus. Except Erin Morales, who clung to him like an older sister the rest of the day– or at least, like a proud aunt. Nelson had purchased a copy of DeLaney's new book for everyone, *Snap Count: Getting your team to move together*.

Anna texted him during lunch, "I hear a star is born. Erin said you were amazing. Proud of you."

Marcus had hoped to talk with Anna tonight, but his call a few minutes earlier was picked up by her voice mail. His phone rang as he continued to clutch it while he resumed walking. The caller ID announced Teresa Younger.

"Hey, Teresa. To what do I owe this pleasure?" Marcus was upbeat.

"You're famous, Buzz. Heard you killed this morning. I knew you would."

"Thanks. I was pleased . . . and relieved . . .with how it went. How'd you hear so fast?"

"Are you kidding? I'm connected. Besides Ballard called during lunch and told me. I asked him to give me a report."

"You have eyes everywhere, don't you?" Marcus joked.

"You should have Facebooked it. Or at least tweeted something about it."

"You know I've never quite gotten into all that," Marcus reminded.

"Yeah, I know. But that's about to change, Buzz. We're going to get you connected. You're going to be a legend by the time I'm done," Teresa boasted.

"I'm not sure I'm legend material."

"You underestimate yourself, Marcus, dear. Am I not getting through to you?"

"This is all so overwhelming. Over the last two weeks it seems like everyone is trying to remake me into some kind of a super hero. Speech coaching, fashion consultant, dress rehearsals," Marcus said.

"Wait. Who's been doing this coaching and consulting?" Teresa queried.

"Marcy Capshaw. You know. Someone I met through Elliot Sloan when we were putting our team presentation together."

"Do I need to check her out?" Teresa sounded wary.

"Why would you need to do that?" Marcus asked.

"It's tough enough going up against a mysterious attorney from Springfield who has some kind of a spell on you. I'm just curious. That's all."

"In that case, Marcy is no worry to you. She's a good ten years older, and it's strictly professional," Marcus assured.

"If you say so," Teresa turned serious. "But someday, you'll realize what's standing right in front of you in plain sight, Marcus Winn."

Marcus was quiet.

Teresa continued," But, hey, today you're a star . . . and I'm proud of you, and I want to celebrate with you. Let me fix you dinner Sunday night when you get back. I'm a hell of a cook. Just no one knows that side of me around here. Come on. What do you say?" she insisted.

Marcus hesitated mulling over the offer, "Ummmmmm. OK. You're on. Text me your address," Marcus agreed. "But no strings attached. Right?"

"Sure. No strings attached," Teresa agreed. "I'll fix my specialty."

"Sounds like a deal. I'll see you then," Marcus concluded.

Teresa said good night and ended the call.

Well, that was certainly unexpected. Hope I'm not starting something I can't finish . . . not getting in too deep. Can't say I'm not interested, though. If it weren't for Anna, I probably would have said yes to Teresa weeks ago. She's persistent. That's for sure.

Marcus slipped his phone into his pants pocket and turned his attention up the shoreline. A tall figure approached. Marcus couldn't make out who it was at first, then realized it was Nelson Johnstone. Nelson walked as if he were on a mission.

"Marcus, is that you?" Nelson's voice was unmistakable.

"Yes sir," Marcus answered. "Are you out for a stroll, too?"

"I thought I saw you coming this way and decided to see if I could catch you alone . . . For that talk I promised this morning," Nelson replied.

"Sure. Glad you did," Marcus agreed enthusiastically. "This is a good place for it."

Nelson pointed up the slope to a group of benches, "Let's go up there where we can relax for a few minutes," Nelson suggested and started walking. Marcus followed.

"DeLaney is quite a coach, isn't he?" Nelson started off as they neared the benches.

"I enjoyed the story about his come-from-behind win for the conference championship and a trip to the Super Bowl," Marcus agreed.

"Quite a story. I can relate to his half-time talk about how the team seemed to have just forgotten how to play football. Simple stuff like blocking, tackling, and holding onto the football," Nelson chuckled. "All he had to do was help them refocus. They had the passion to win. They had the best record in the NFL that season. They just forgot to play with clarity, read the keys they had practiced, cover their part of the play, and be alert how to help a teammate when possible. Basic stuff."

"The basics are the basics, whether it's the NFL or the local ten-and-under soccer league. Right?" Marcus added.

"Right," Nelson echoed as he reached the benches and motioned for Marcus to take a seat next to him.

"Tell me, Marcus, what are your thoughts on your speech this morning?" Nelson asked.

"I was nervous about coming up this weekend, but I knew I had been coached well and was as prepared as I could be. All-in-all, I am pleased. I was a little surprised by the ovation, but flattered," Marcus tried to undersell how elated he actually was with his performance.

"Fair enough," Nelson nodded several times as he paused. "You really impressed Patty and Lizzy–especially Lizzy–and they are hard to impress."

"They both came up to me during lunch and hugged me," Marcus admitted. "I didn't know quite how to react."

"I was already impressed with you, Marcus, but not because of anything you said–which was excellent, by the way," Nelson went on. Marcus sat quietly. Nelson continued.

"What impressed me was the way your team responded back in March to the funding presentation. When they entered the conference room in force, I could see the passion in their eyes. As you presented, I watched the faces of your team—their expressions. It was obvious to me that they had the utmost confidence in you and respect for you. It was that, as much as the presentation, that told me you all deserved every chance I could give you to succeed. I didn't want to give up on you, or the project, or my dream of incorporating alternative energy into our product mix."

Marcus spoke, "Like I said when you came down to the lab, it was a team effort. All I had to do was create the space where they could perform."

"As far as the speech. I thought it was brilliant . . . simply brilliant," Nelson reached and patted Marcus on his knee for emphasis.

"Thank you, sir. That means a lot to me," Marcus couldn't help but smile.

"I'd like to ask how you would feel about letting me use the video of your presentation to promote some leadership ideas in our company. I know I could just go ahead and use the video, but somehow, I thought I should ask first, out of respect for your personal stories," Nelson said.

"I'd be honored. How do you think you could use them?" Marcus was curious.

"I think I want everyone in the company to see your speech in its entirety. So, I'd have Beverly promote it through the Derrick and post a link to it," Nelson said.

"I think that would be fine," Marcus agreed.

"Then, I'd like to take the six main points you made, edit the video to highlight each point, and use each one as the main theme of an individual segment to train our managers about leadership. Patty wrote down those main points and gave them to me after the session. She told me I was missing an opportunity if I didn't do something with them," Nelson explained.

"Wow. I'm uh . . . I'm uh . . . I'm speechless," Marcus gave up a nervous chuckle. But he had reservations, "How do you think it will go over? I'm sure not everyone would agree with my ideas," Marcus asked.

"I'm not concerned about that, Marcus. I'm thinking ahead. I know there's other new supervisors like you who are anxious to move up. Frankly, most of the senior managers will probably be retired in the next ten years. I've got to think about the next wave of leaders. People like Erin, and you, and any number of young people on staff who are eager and talented, waiting for their turn. I don't think they should have to wait. Do you?"

"No sir, I don't." Marcus agreed excitedly.

"Good. Then it's settled. I need to discuss this with a couple of people first. I'd appreciate it if you would keep a lid on it around the office until I get back with you next week. Agreed?"

"Agreed."

Nelson stood up, "Better get back. I didn't tell Patty I was going out. She'll be sending out a search party soon."

Nelson took a couple of steps toward the trail leading to the mansion, then turned around, "One more thing, Marcus."

"Sir?"

"ReEnergizing America's Future isn't just about energy. It's not just a PR slogan or tag line like most people think—even most of my vice presidents and department heads. I think, according to Elliot, you called them the, '*Halobs*, hairy-legged-old-boys?' For some reason, that term has stuck in my head. I think it's hilarious."

"I didn't mean any disrespect," Marcus apologized.

"I know you didn't, Marcus. But it's true that the old way of leading and doing things is not good enough any more. There are so many talented and eager young people like you coming on. I'm excited for your generation, and I wish all my halob friends could get past their fear of change and embrace all this creative energy," Nelson sounded hopeful.

"Thank you, sir. I'm glad to hear you say that," Marcus smiled and nodded.

Nelson continued, "ReEnergizing America's Future. To me it's about reenergizing the American spirit of discovery, and enterprise, and community—the spirit that built this country.

"I'm afraid that somehow we've let it slip away since I took over the company from my dad. In America, we've reduced everything to spreadsheets and the sacred bottom line. All the fun and adventure has been sucked out. Profit margins and dividend checks have replaced passion. I think if we're only focused on the bottom line, we're aiming way too low.

JEE Mission Statement
"ReEnergizing America's Future"

"Profit margins and dividend checks have replaced passion. I think if we're only focused on the bottom line, we're aiming too low."

~Nelson Johnstone

"That's why I've resisted taking the company public. I still believe Johnstone Enterprises can be an example of how America can regain that spirit, get reenergized from its core. Not everyone gets that, but I sense that you do,"

Nelson paused. Marcus nodded once to acknowledge message received. "Good night, son." Nelson turned and disappeared up the trail.

Marcus sat quietly for several minutes letting everything that just happened soak in.

He retrieved his phone. 11:02 p.m. popped up on the screen. Marcus tapped the call button anyway. The call was answered on the third ring.

"Hi, Dad. You're not going to believe the kind of day I had today."

10. A new normal

Marcus placed another phone call after breakfast Sunday morning.

"Hi, Mom. Happy Mother's Day," Marcus began. . . .

"Yes, it's been a wonderful weekend . . .

"I'm coming up to Joplin Friday night to spend the weekend at home with you and Dad. I'll fill you in then. OK? . . .

"Anna? She's fine. Busy. I haven't seen her as much lately as I'd like. Lawyer stuff, you know . . .

"I love you, too. You're the greatest Mom ever. I'm glad you and Dad are finally back home to stay. . .

"I will, Mom. I'll be careful. Bye."

The morning sun warmed Marcus's face as he tilted his head and took a slow deep breath. The fragrance of loblolly pine mingled with honeysuckle permeated the dew-saturated air on this second Sunday in May. Marcus felt more relaxed and connected to his surroundings this morning than he had felt in weeks; so he decided to take a leisurely drive along the back roads of northeast Oklahoma on his return trip to Tulsa. Marcus could imagine the caravan of Johnstone employees barreling down the

Will Rogers Turnpike to get back to Tulsa before the Sunday crowds hit the restaurants. He was in no such rush.

The official program wrapped up Saturday night with a reception for Congressman Wakefield at the Phoenix Lodge prior to the concluding banquet, the single dress up occasion of the weekend.

This was Nelson's night. Nelson delivered his traditional state of the company address before presenting several recognitions to individuals for exemplary service to the company and to the community.

And, of course, the various winners of the golf scramble that day were recognized, and awarded their prizes during the dessert course.

Each of the committee members was awarded a reserved front row table for their service. They could invite whomever they chose to join them. Gerald Donovan included Marcus along with Erin Morales, who did not have a plus one for the weekend.

Marcus wondered how many years might pass before he would qualify to attend another JEE leadership retreat.

Marcus finally got to talk with Anna Saturday afternoon, when she took a break from helping a law partner prepare for trial. She apologized profusely for missing his call Friday night, but it was unavoidable. He would have gone into greater detail about everything–the Wilkes House, the speech, the ovation, the conversation with Nelson–the details that brief work breaks do not allow. That would have to wait for another time, another call.

But Jeannie had plenty of time to hear it all, when he called after hanging up with Anna. Jeannie was thrilled her dancing lesson paid off for Marcus, and she was over-joyed that he mentioned her by name in his speech.

"Really?" she exclaimed at the news. "Really? I've never been that important to anyone. Ever! And you said my name to all those executives? And you said it was my idea?" Jeannie could not imagine that her simple dancing lesson had been of such importance.

"Yes I did, and Mrs. Johnstone told me her favorite point was that leaders lead. The leader must take the first step so everyone can move together," Marcus bragged. "Remember? Remember showing me how that worked in the middle of the labyrinth?"

"I remember," Jeannie's voice softened. "You've made my day. No–my week!"

"It doesn't take much to make you happy then," Marcus responded.

"Just knowing that I matter to you, Marcus, makes me happy," Jeannie confessed softly.

"Then, Jeannie Irwin," Marcus said, "you should be elated every day."

The trip home was a windows-down affair. Some-times a convertible seems like a good idea, Marcus thought, as he guided his Z over the winding two-lane highways and eventually across the Pensacola Dam that made Grand Lake possible. He decided to cut back south, after crossing the dam, and go down to the Creek Nation Turnpike before turning west toward Tulsa. He had plenty of time to get home, unpack, shower, and change before going to Teresa's for dinner.

The last forty miles of the trip went faster when Marcus was able to kick his Z up to turnpike speed. Teresa texted her address and promised him a home cooked dinner to remember.

I'm not sure I should have accepted her invitation. Marcus thought. Teresa obviously wants to be more than friends. But we have boundaries. I'm sure it will be OK. . . Still. . . But Anna said we have that freedom. At least until we decide to make an exclusive commitment. I guess I shouldn't feel guilty about anything. . . Still. And I really do want to celebrate this with someone who cares. I know Teresa will be eager to hear every little detail.

But Marcus knew he couldn't tell everyone everything about what had happened. For now, he couldn't tell anyone about the details of his Friday night private talk with Nelson.

He probably shouldn't tell anyone yet about his casual encounter with Lizzy on the Wilkes House second floor balcony last night. That she told him how she and Travis had become instant fans. They wished he would accept their invitation to their cookout Memorial Day, and bring a plus-one. Anna came immediately to mind.

He wasn't sure how much he should say about a brief private conversation with Congressman Wakefield at his reception. The Congressman said he wanted to know more about his wind project from someone with front line experience, not an executive lobbying for funding. Would Marcus be open to a discreet meeting next time the Congressman was back in Tulsa? No fanfare.

He probably shouldn't go on too much about some of the comments and compliments he received from several executives. One person in particular, Lane McConley, bordered on overboard with his lavish praise for Marcus within earshot of several V-Ps and Nelson. McConley introduced himself as part of the asset development team connected to both Martin Slater and to Wally Pierce, the corporate Chief Strategic Development Officer. McConley said, so everyone could hear, that he could tell Marcus, "would be an important leader in the company someday," and that he, McConley, was there to help Marcus any way he could. Just call on him anytime. That said, McConley was off to play in the golf scramble, which his team won, by-the-way.

The people with whom Marcus was most eager to share his experience, however, were his project team. That would happen first thing in the morning. He had already discussed some ideas with Dan Packwood, and asked Dan to alert everyone that he wanted to take a few extra minutes during the huddle to present them.

* * *

Marcus reviewed the key six points of his presentation in his head during the brief commute to work Monday morning:

1. Everyone is already motivated to want to win.

2. Clarity of vision produces clarity of purpose and action.

3. It's my job as team leader to provide a safe place where my team can grow.

4. Everyone matters. We all have hopes, dreams, expectations, and disappointments. Every person is inherently valuable, without exception.

5. Leaders lead. My team is looking to me to take the first step.

6. A leader provides a safe environment for honest two-way communication.

Marcus intended to share these points with his team. He would make a personal commitment to them that he would create and protect the team environment so they could express the creative energy of their personal IN-Powerment in the way they contributed. He wanted the Burns Flat project team lab to be the model of this new way to lead, and he wanted them to know he was so proud of them that he could just pop.

Marcus entered the lab at 7:50 a.m., as usual. The aroma of brewing coffee greeted him, as usual. He could hear the laughter and bantering conversation coming from the break area, as usual. He flipped on the lights to his office, dropped off his leather messenger bag, and headed back toward the break area.

It looked like everyone was back there. He even saw Dan and Sierra, which was a little unusual, standing in front of the gathering. As he reached the group, all had turned to face him coming up the corridor. Miranda stepped forward to greet him with a hot cup of herbal tea. Spontaneous applause and cheering erupted. The crowd parted to reveal a giant cookie covered in icing with the inscription, "So proud we could pop."

* * *

It had been the kind of week where everything was in that state of flow. Marcus noticed that the level of interaction among the team had picked up—more than he could remember in the past. There was an ease about them and among them he had not seen before. Even Brad interacted more; although, others usually initiated it with him instead of the other way around. At least he wasn't sitting in his office with the door closed most of the time, as before. That was a plus in Marcus's book.

He had spoken with Anna three out of the four previous nights, resuming their usual 9:30 p.m. phone date. They didn't talk as long, but at least they talked—mostly about work. Marcus thanked Anna for telling him about Eric Greer's "room appeal." Marcus had taken Greer's storytelling example to heart and realized he used a similar technique in his own speech. Marcus never mentioned his conversations with Congressman Wakefield, other than say he got to meet the Congressman at the reception.

Anna still planned to go with Marcus to Jeannie's high school graduation next Thursday. Marcus planned to stay over until Saturday before returning to Tulsa for the Frisk's Memorial Day cookout on Sunday.

Anna wasn't sure she could make it to the cookout. Memorial Day is an important fund raising weekend for the campaign, and she had been assigned to the finance team. She might have to attend an event, but she would try to wiggle out of it.

Marcus chose not to bring up June the first. Neither did Anna.

Marcus lunched at Teresa's table twice that week. Ten could crowd around. There were two regulars with Teresa: Lily, Teresa's office mate, and Chad, the geologist. Faces in the other six places changed each time. Marcus got the definite impression that Teresa orchestrated who occupied those spots. That's probably why she would call each morning before 9:00 a.m. to ask if he planned to lunch with her. "Just checking," she would say. She always sat on Marcus's right. Her demeanor toward him continued as it had been–friendly, but appropriately professional; although, they both knew it could easily be more than that.

Marcy had Marcus over Tuesday evening for pizza–her treat–to review his speech video. Beverly Trudeau was there, too. Marcus did not realize Marcy and Beverly were good friends, or that Marcy's connections with JEE ran so deep.

When Marcus asked about paying Marcy for her services, she just said not to worry; it had been taken care of. Nelson had briefed Beverly about the leadership training idea, and she was already working up some preliminary information with Jerry from HR. Planning would begin in earnest after Memorial Day.

Marcus would be brought in officially at that time to be part of the leadership development team. They liked his INPowerment terminology and wanted to get his permission to use it. All that would be decided later with Marcus's involvement. They could see the potential in this program. They also wanted to involve someone prominent from the oil and gas side, but just who, had not been decided. There were several possibilities.

Congressman Wakefield's field office had called to confirm Marcus was still interested in meeting with the Congressman. That meeting would likely be around the July 4th holiday, when the Congressman would be in Tulsa.   They would work out the details closer to the date.

What a ride, Marcus thought. *What a ride it has been since early October. All I wanted was to be a great engineer like my dad. I just wanted to harness the power of wind. I wonder what would have happened if Erin hadn't called me in to coach me about my supervising? If my job hadn't been on the line, would I have reacted to Anna differently? Would I have gone for that walk around the lake to work things out? Would I have missed out on meeting Jeannie altogether? Would I have ever thought twice about walking the labyrinth? Would I have asked for a mentor and become friends with Elliot? Blows my mind to think about all the other ways this could have gone.*

But it worked out this way.

All these possibilities opening up in front of me. My life is getting larger. I would have never thought that I could stand in front of an audience and speak as I did at the retreat. I would have never known how much I would like the rush of it. I would have never imagined that I could become a leader within my company as a whole. That Nelson Johnstone, himself, would sit on a lakeside bench with me in the middle of the night and tell me he thinks I get it. I get what he means by ReEnergizing America's Future. The same way he does.

I would have never imagined that a sitting Congressman, my Congressman, a real Congressman, not a congressman wannabe, would ask me for a private meeting to get my advice. Me! Marcus Winn.

There have been so many people who have encouraged me. They have certainly generated a new spirit in me. Like Nelson said, "ReEnergizing the spirit." They made me believe that I could, by believing in me.

Elliot, Erin, Anna, Lauren, Jeannie, Jarod, even Andy and Susie have taught me lessons I needed. They enlightened me when I definitely needed to learn how to work with people and think like a leader. Each gave me information and insights through their own life experience that helped me see what I needed to do next.

Then, there's Jeannie. What a spirit. Not only does she have the right thing to say to me at the right time, like no one else, but every time I'm around her I walk away happier and more energized. She makes me feel so alive. She enlivens my heart. I hope I do the same for her. I can hardly wait to see what kind of a young woman she grows into. I'm sure she's going to amaze us all.

Marcy and Teresa have opened me up to the possibilities out there through networking and connecting. I don't know how I drifted into my own small "Marcus world," but

I'm excited about branching out, and I'm thankful they came along to drag me out of it.

Yeah, Marcus Winn. It has been a wild ride. Hang on.

* * *

Marcus felt out of place on the oil and gas side of the building, especially in the drilling department's suite. Marcus wondered if he should be carrying a white flag since he had "single-handedly ruined their chance," of taking over Millennium's wing when Millennium lost funding, as they were counting on. But thanks to Marcus, that hadn't worked out like it was supposed to for drilling.

It didn't take Marcus long to locate his destination in the suite. The cubicles were well labeled with each occupant's name and title.

Marcus knocked on the metal trim to announce his presence. The startled occupant lurched around in his swivel chair.

"So, this is where Jim Bob Danner works," Marcus began.

"Yeah, what's it to you?" Jim Bob scowled as he stood to claim his space.

"Just wondered what the son of a legend looks like," Marcus continued.

"Wha d'ya mean?" Danner asked.

"I hear you're Archie Danner's boy. Did I get that right?"

"So?" Jim Bob straightened up.

"Hell of a driller. Archie."

"Yes he was, I'm proud to say."

"People say you might be as good some day."

"Better." Jim Bob corrected. "So, why are you here, wind boy?"

"Professional curiosity, Jim Bob, professional curiosity," Marcus answered.

"How so?"

"If I'm going to be part of an oil and gas company, I need to know more about it. Wouldn't you agree?" Marcus continued.

"Would seem like a good idea," Jim Bob retorted.

"So, I came to learn. Since you are the best driller around here, I thought you would be the best one to teach me."

"Now, why would I want to waste my time with you?" Jim Bob's head tilted to the right as he crossed his arms and widened his stance during the asking of the question.

"No reason you should. Just thought you might like to show off a little. Show a wind boy why roughnecks have a reputation for being so tough."

"Think you have what it takes to run with my crowd?" Jim Bob challenged.

"I'll do my best to keep up. Maybe you can toughen me up a little," Marcus admitted.

"Got a hard hat?" Jim Bob asked.

"Got one," Marcus answered.

"Got steel toed boots?"

"Yep."

"Can you get away for a few days. I'm going to Montana mid June to check on some wells up there. Can you tag along?"

"I can arrange it."

"I'll have to approve it with Aaron Jackson, my V-P."

"I'll hear back from you, then? Right?" Marcus clarified.

"Yeah. Next week some time."

"Good," Marcus said.

"OK," Jim Bob answered.

Marcus turned to walk away.

"Hey," Jim Bob called out. Marcus stopped and turned. Jim Bob had walked to his cubicle doorway where Marcus had been standing. "Hardly seems natural that a wind boy would want to learn about drilling up close and personal. Not a normal thing."

"Well, then," Marcus spoke through a wide smile as he turned squarely to Jim Bob, "we better get used to a new normal."

Marcus turned and stepped into his unexpected future. . .

WITH A NEW WAY TO LEAD.

Discussion & application questions

The following discussion questions will help you apply Marcus Winn's story in your own life, both personally and at work. We experience life the same way Marcus does, one day at a time and through our own eyes.

The questions are designed to make you think how you would react if you were in Marcus's place and how you can transfer what you observe and learn from his experience to your own.

Think of the ways you can make *Marcus Winn's workplace story of an INPowering life* real for you in one or more of the following ways:

1. Individual application through self-study and self-reflection,
2. Discussion in reading groups in your organization or with like minded friends,
3. Training and continuing education around the skills Marcus is learning.

Now, continue.

1. Fighting Words

1. Marcus is becoming more widely known in Johnstone Energy Enterprises because of his recent success leading his team to save funding for their projects. Jim Bob called him a, "celebrity." How do we treat celebrities different than non-celebrities?

2. Celebrity power is only one source of power for Marcus. What other forms of power does he have? *(page 8)*

3. Who are the celebrities in your organization? What did they do to become a celebrity?

4. Elliot Sloan is Marcus's mentor within the company. What is your impression of Marcus's relationship with Elliot?

5. What is your impression of Jim Bob Danner?

6. Jim Bob has a specific perspective from which he forms his opinions of the way things should be. What is it?

7. How might different perspectives, or points of view, contribute to conflicts?

8. Jim Bob's insults provoked Marcus's urge to defend himself. What is your reaction when others provoke you, insult you, or in any way stir your emotions to retaliate? How do you handle that provocation?

9. How did Marcus's response affect his "power"?

10. Why is Marcus anxious about his upcoming presentation?

2. Reality check

1. Marcus continually seeks out quiet places for reflection. What role does reflection play in your approach to handling daily issues?

2. Do you agree with Marcus that maybe he should not have been so quick to accept Gerald Donovan's invitation to make a presentation at the corporate leadership retreat? Explain.

3. Marcus reflected on how several individuals had contributed to his recent success without them realizing how important their role had been. How much of what we learn comes from such incidental interactions compared to the "formal" education we receive?

4. As he thinks about his upcoming presentation, Marcus realizes he has a team backing him up. When we face an individual crisis, how can a support group help us through it? How likely are we to hesitate calling on help? Why do you think that is?

5. Teresa makes a pertinent observation about Marcus. What is it? What is her suggestion to remedy it?

6. How would you describe the current relationship Marcus has with his work team?

7. What's the story behind how the Monday huddle evolved? What routines have your work group developed that are now part of the team culture? How do those routines contribute to the team's performance?

8. How important was the "invitation to join" to Marcus's decision to lunch with Teresa and her group?

9. Marcus drafted his questions to understand what motivated his team at work and what they considered important to leadership. What is your assessment of his questions? What other questions would you ask?

10. A vested interest is a personal reason for wanting something to be done. What is Gerald Donovan's vested interest in Marcus presenting at the leadership retreat?

11. What is Jim Bob Danner's vested interest in wanting Millennium Energy to fail?

12. What role do vested interests play in decisions we make or in what we ask others to do?

3. Team debrief

1. Why was Marcus surprised by Sue Ann's insistence on leading the debriefing session?

2. What was Sue Ann's reasons for wanting to lead the meeting?

3. What would you expect Marcus to learn about his own situation from Sue Ann's example?

4. What impact do you think Marcus's response to Sue Ann's facilitation of the meeting had on Sue Ann? The team as a whole?

5. What did Marcus do so effectively in the way he praised Sue Ann?

6. Why was Dan Packwood pleased with Marcus's handling of the debriefing session? How do you think that affected their relationship?

4. Crash course

1. How does Marcus use Elliot as a mentor?

2. What does Elliot say to help Marcus deal with his encounter with Jim Bob Danner?

3. Elliot tells Marcus, "the worst thing that can happen to a leader is being ignored." What message do you get from that comment?

4. What was the "reality check" Elliot offered to Marcus?

5. How do Elliot's comments to Marcus compare with what Teresa told him earlier?

6. How did Marcus use Jim Bob as a challenge to his own sense of empowerment?

7. In what ways would you consider Elliot's comments to Marcus to be a "crash course?"

8. Notice when Marcus asked about Marcy, Elliot did not volunteer to call her for him. What do you think Elliot was saying to Marcus by pushing Marcus to initiate the call?

9. How did Elliot help Marcus reframe the objective of his presentation at the leadership retreat?

10. Marcy interacted with Marcus as a coach. What was the difference in the tone of her interaction with Marcus compared to Elliot's earlier mentoring conversation with Marcus?

11. Describe your impression of Marcy and the point in life where she finds herself.

Chapter 5. Straight talk

1. Everyone on Marcus's team emailed their responses to his questionnaire except Brad, who delivered them in a written note placed in an envelope on Marcus's desk. If you were Marcus, how would you interpret Brad's action?

2. Marcus tabulates the responses from his team. What is your take on the responses and Marcus's reaction to them?

3. How does the team's responses to motivators and leadership characteristics compare to yours? What would you add?

4. How does Marcus's experience with being prepared to make his speech compare to what Anna is experiencing as she works with a candidate for the U.S. House of Representatives?

5. Anna tells Marcus that Eric Greer is, "an amazing storyteller." How have you been influenced by stories from leaders in you decisions to join a cause or to support a leader?

6. Marcus is confronting several "realities" in his professional and personal life. How do you think confronting these realities will affect his growth as a leader?

6. Dance lesson

1. What is your impression of how Marcy is preparing Marcus for his presentation?

2. What do you think Marcus is learning from the development process?

3. What role does Marcus's self-reflection play in his learning?

4. What role does self-awareness through self-reflection play in your own personal growth?

5. What impact does learning he will be staying at the Wilkes House have on Marcus's state of mind?

6. Marcus solicited information from his team in writing and in individual interviews. What did Marcus hope to learn in the individual interviews? If you were in Marcus's position, how comfortable would you be that his team was sincere in their responses? Explain.

7. What is your take on the connection that Marcus is developing with Jeannie?

8. What did Jeannie do to improve her relationship with Johnny, her younger brother?

9. What is Marcus learning about Jeannie as he becomes more acquainted with her?

10. What similarities to you see between Marcus and Jeannie as they enter their respective transitional life experiences?

11. What does Jeannie say about an artist's perspective? What examples did she give? How did she use her examples to challenge Marcus?

12. What leadership lessons did Jeannie share with Marcus using dancing as an analogy?

13. Why did Marcus think Jeannie's dance lesson was, "good stuff"?

7. On site

1. How does Marcus continue his preparation during his drive to the retreat?

2. What role does mental rehearsal play in preparation? How do you use it?

3. From your understanding of the dress rehearsal Marcy staged for Marcus, what do you think Marcy might have in mind for Marcus in the future?

4. How would you compare the expectations Gerald Donovan had for Marcus's presentation and Marcus's expectations?

5. In leading, what might happen when the expectations of the leaders and the expectations of the team are not aligned?

6. What is the value in Marcus's strategy to, "under promise and over deliver"?

7. How did Elliot see Marcus's opportunity at the retreat?

8. In your circle of acquaintances, who are the, "connectors"?

9. We learn that Marcus learned to seek out advice from Erin. How comfortable do you feel seeking out advice from your supervisor? If you are a supervisor, how often do your team members seek advice from you?

10. What is your impression of Nelson and Patty Johnstone from the way they welcomed Marcus at the Wilkes House?

11. What effect do you think staying at the Wilkes House had on Marcus's celebrity power at the retreat?

12. What did you learn about Millennium Energy from the interaction between Tony Preston and Randall Allenbaugh?

13. What was the value to Marcus for hearing that interaction and sharing that ride to the dinner with them?

14. Why was it important that Marcy follow up with Marcus the night before his presentation?

15. What lessons about coaching do you get from Marcy's attention to Marcus?

8. Center stage

1. What was the value of Marcus's morning jog before his presentation?

2. What routines do you have that center you before important events?

3. What are your impressions of the encouragement messages Marcus received before his presentation?

4. What did you learn about the audience from Marcus's observation of the meeting room? What does that suggest about Johnstone Enterprises?

5. How did Marcus reflect the impact of Marcy's coaching as he took his place center stage?

6. Discuss your impressions of Marcus's speech and what you learned about leadership from it.

7. What is your take on Marcus's definition of a leader?

8. Why did Marcus choose to remake the term, "empowerment," into "INPowerment"?

9. What is your take on Marcus's point that his opportunity as a leader is to help, "unleash the creative energy of personal INPowerment"?

10. What do you think is the proper balance between being people oriented, clear minded, and performance driven?

11. What role do boundaries play in establishing and maintaining a corporate culture?

12. According to Marcus, who is responsible for establishing those boundaries?

13. How do you think you might have reacted to it if you had been sitting in the audience?

14. Marcus told Marcy he wanted Millennium to be more respected in Johnstone Enterprises. How successful do you think he was he in accomplishing that?

15. What impact did making the speech have on Marcus himself?

16. Put yourself in the places of Elliot, Erin, Donovan, and the Millennium Energy delegation. What do you think was going through their minds as they listened to Marcus?

17. If you had been one of those pulling for the failure of Millennium Energy, what might you be thinking by the end of Marcus's presentation?

18. How does Marcus's new way to lead compare your own ideas about leading?

9. After glow

1. Were you surprised to learn that no "Jim Bobs" showed up in the Q & A following Marcus's speech? Why?

2. What do you make of how word got out so quickly to non-attenders about Marcus's performance?

3. What does it say about Teresa's influence that the VP of her department would report on Marcus's speech to her, or that she would feel comfortable asking him to do so?

4. What was Teresa's promise to Marcus when she talked to him later that night? Why do you think she is so interested in promoting Marcus?

5. What did you learn about Nelson Johnstone from his conversation with Marcus late Friday night?

6. What lesson about leading and winning did Nelson and Marcus take away from Jackson DeLaney's after dinner speech?

7. What did Nelson say was the first thing that got his attention about Marcus? How might that have affected the way he listened to Marcus's presentation?

8. What opportunity did Nelson see about how to use Marcus's speech to benefit the whole company?

9. What impact did that information have on Marcus?

10. What did Nelson think about his company's mission statement?

11. What has to happen for a mission statement to become engrained in the rank-and-file of the organization?

12. What impact do you think Marcus's speech had on Nelson personally?

13. What does Nelson's attitude toward change seem to be for his company? How might Marcus fit it to the change process?

14. What does it say about Marcus's relationship with his dad that he would want to tell him about his experience at the end of the day? How does this relate to his earlier comparison of his relationships with Elliot as

a corporate mentor, and his dad as a life mentor? Can
we have more than one mentor at a time?

10. A new normal

1. Marcus wondered when he might be qualified to attend the leadership retreat again. Why do you think
   that would cross his mind?

2. What was the difference between the conversations
   Marcus was able to have on Saturday with Anna and
   Jeannie?

3. Why did Marcus feel relatively comfortable accepting
   Teresa's invitation to dinner Sunday night?

4. Based on what Marcus is reluctant to discuss further
   with others, how has Marcus's position in Johnstone
   Enterprises changed as a result of his presentation?

5. What do you make of the way Lane McConley sought
   out Marcus to compliment him?

6. How did preparing for his speech help Marcus shape
   his, "new way to lead"?

7. How would you expect to see the main points Marcus
   made in his speech play out in how he leads the team
   going forward?

8. How would you describe the health of his team from
   the way they welcomed him to the lab on Monday
   morning?

9. What does the inscription on Marcus's cookie suggest
   about the flow of information in the company?

10. What did Marcus learn about how the company was
    moving forward on Nelson's intention to use Marcus's
    speech for leadership training?

11. Why was it important for Marcus to reach out to Jim
    Bob Danner at the end?

12. What do you think might be going through Jim Bob's mind as Marcus walks away?

13. What do you think the, "new normal," is for Marcus?

Additional discussion questions

1. What parallels do you see between what is happening to Marcus within Johnstone Enterprises, and Eric Greer as a political candidate?

2. Part of INPowering leadership is helping others to enlarge (INLarge) their expectations of living. How do you see this happening for Marcus, Jeannie, Sue Ann and others?

3. What parallels do you see between Nelson seeking out Marcus and Marcus seeking out Jim Bob?

4. What do you see in Marcus's future at Johnstone Enterprises?

5. What is your impression of the impact key women have on Marcus's development? Discuss Anna, Erin, Teresa, Jeannie, Marcy, and Lauren.

6. What effect do you think Millennium Energy will have on the future of Johnstone Oil & Gas?

7. Compare and contrast the concept of "tough love" with Marcus's "new way to lead."

8. Why is important to understand Marcus's personal life in relation to his professional life?

9. Marcus never said his new way was the right way to lead, only that it was what he learned for himself that was helpful. How do we go about deciding how we will lead?

10. How does your way to lead compare with Marcus's?

11. What will you do differently to become a more INPowering leader?

Acknowledgements

This series would not be possible if it were not for the "true believers" who have encouraged me every step of the way. They have offered their insights into human nature and leadership, as well as being a source of inspiration to help me write better. My special thanks to Lynda Atkins, Billy Bailey, Rick Bedlion, and Linda Thomas for always being there for me.

I especially thank Marie Piet for telling every client she meets about the Marcus Winn series. Also, for looking over my shoulder and offering feedback on the manuscript: Kelly Crowe, Kyle Eastham, Megan Hale, and Terri Klouda.

About the author

Garland C. McWatters

is a storyteller, author, and trainer. His passion is to create **IN-Powering** workplaces populated by **INPowered** leaders and contributors.

Garland has enjoyed a variety of professional experiences including broadcasting, journalism, public relations, education, sales, and the ministry. Since 1994, Garland has written and presented training programs in management, leadership, and work process. He has worked from the shop floor to the corporate boardroom in a variety of businesses and organizations of all sizes. His work has taken him to manufacturing of all kinds; information technology; local, county, and state government; financial institutions; insurance; distribution centers; educational institutions; public relations; marketing, and aviation.

Learn more about Garland and his work.

website: www.inpoweredtolead.com.
blog: www.inpoweredtolead.wordpress.com

Proof

Made in the USA
Charleston, SC
19 April 2014